T0115757

ORPHAN BLACK

THE OFFICIAL COLORING BOOK

INSIGHT EDITIONS

San Rafael, California

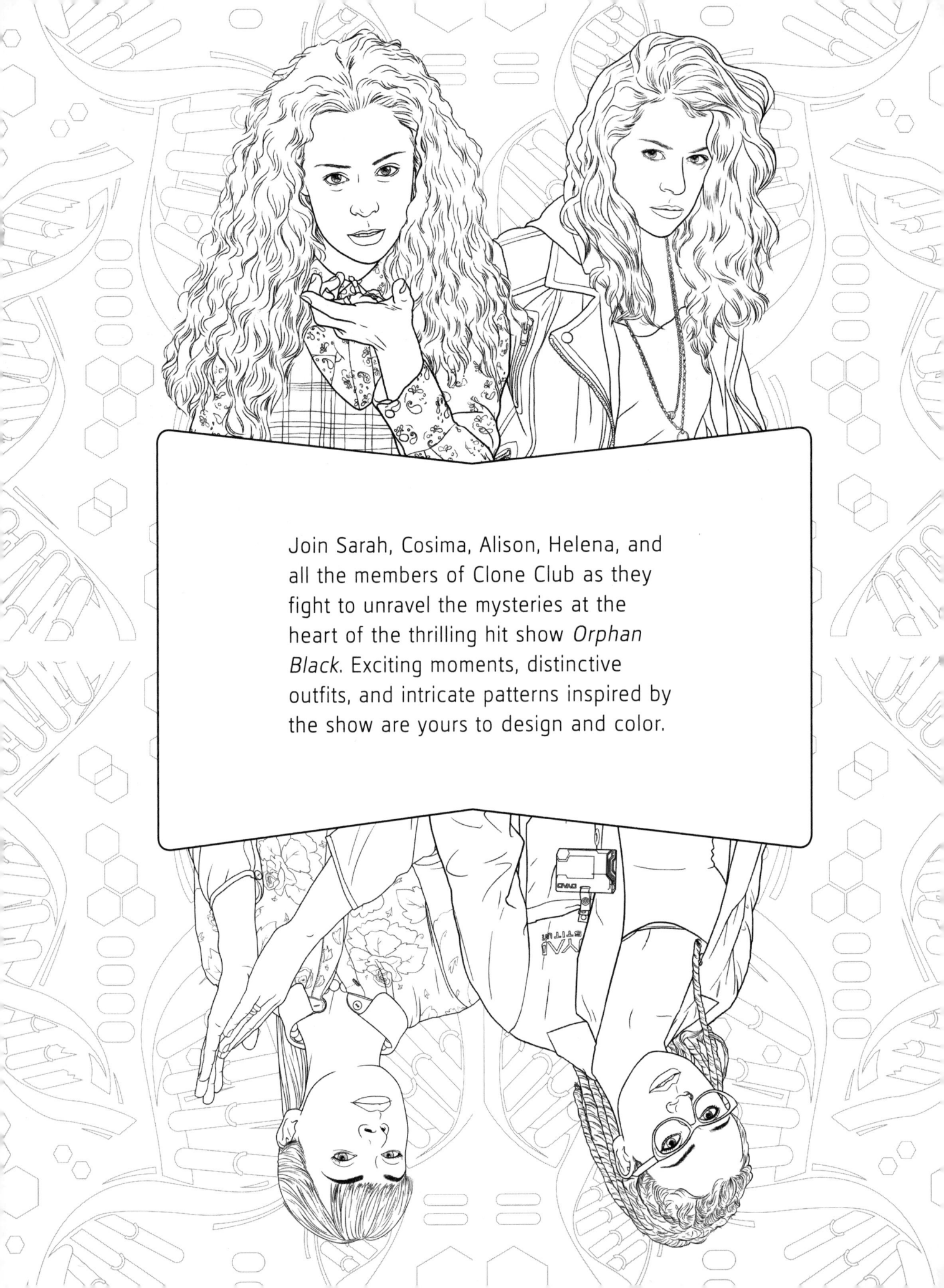

Join Sarah, Cosima, Alison, Helena, and all the members of Clone Club as they fight to unravel the mysteries at the heart of the thrilling hit show *Orphan Black*. Exciting moments, distinctive outfits, and intricate patterns inspired by the show are yours to design and color.

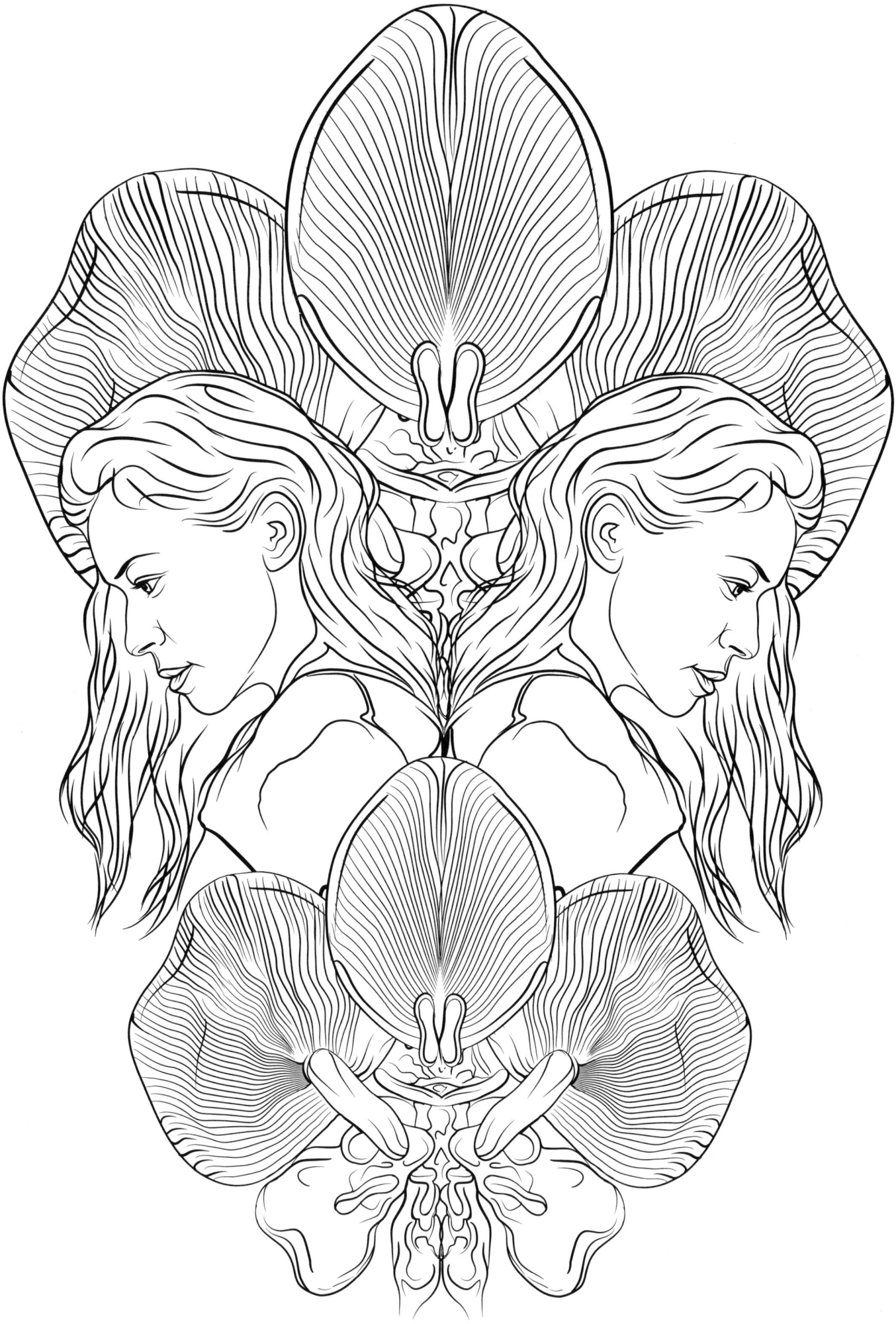

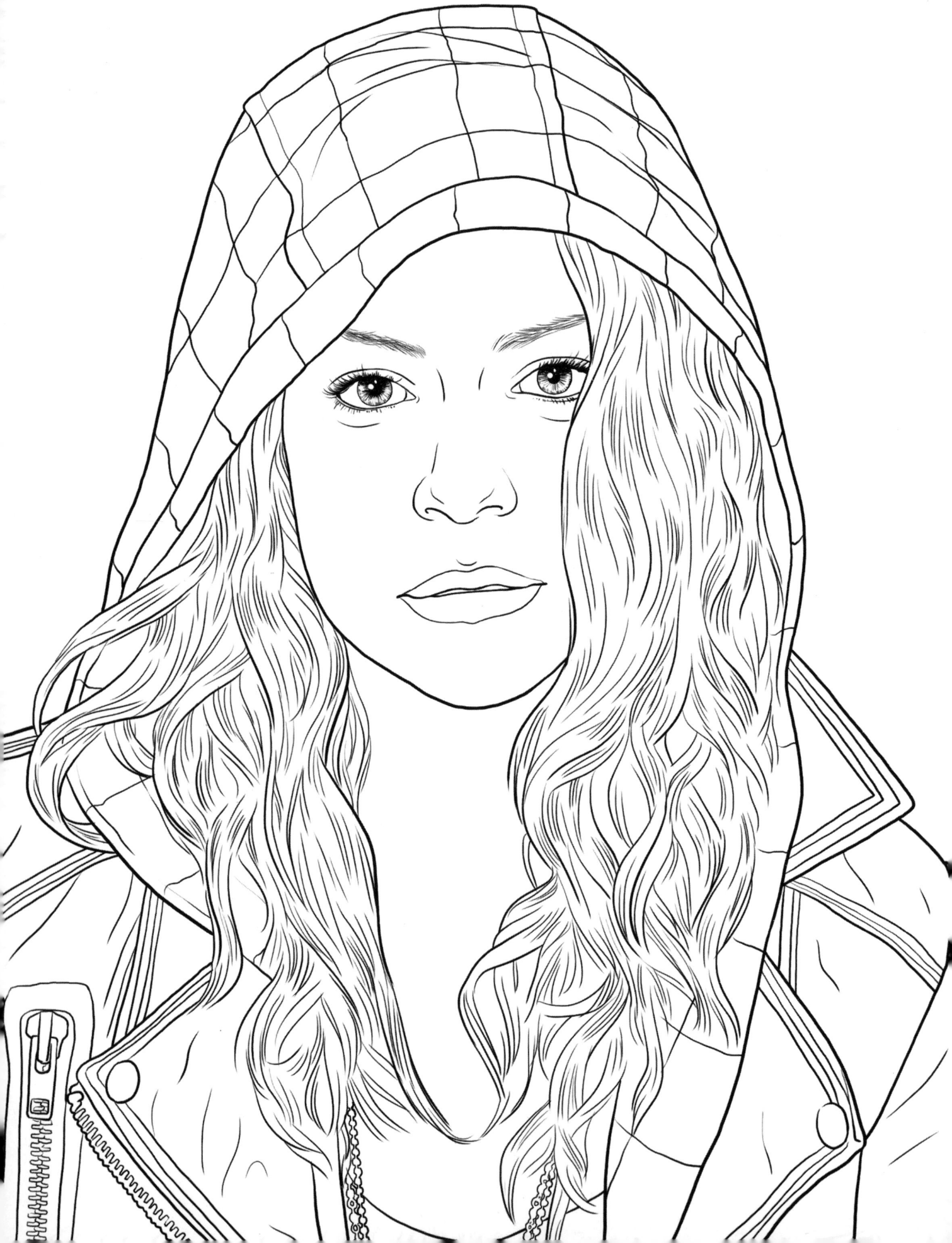

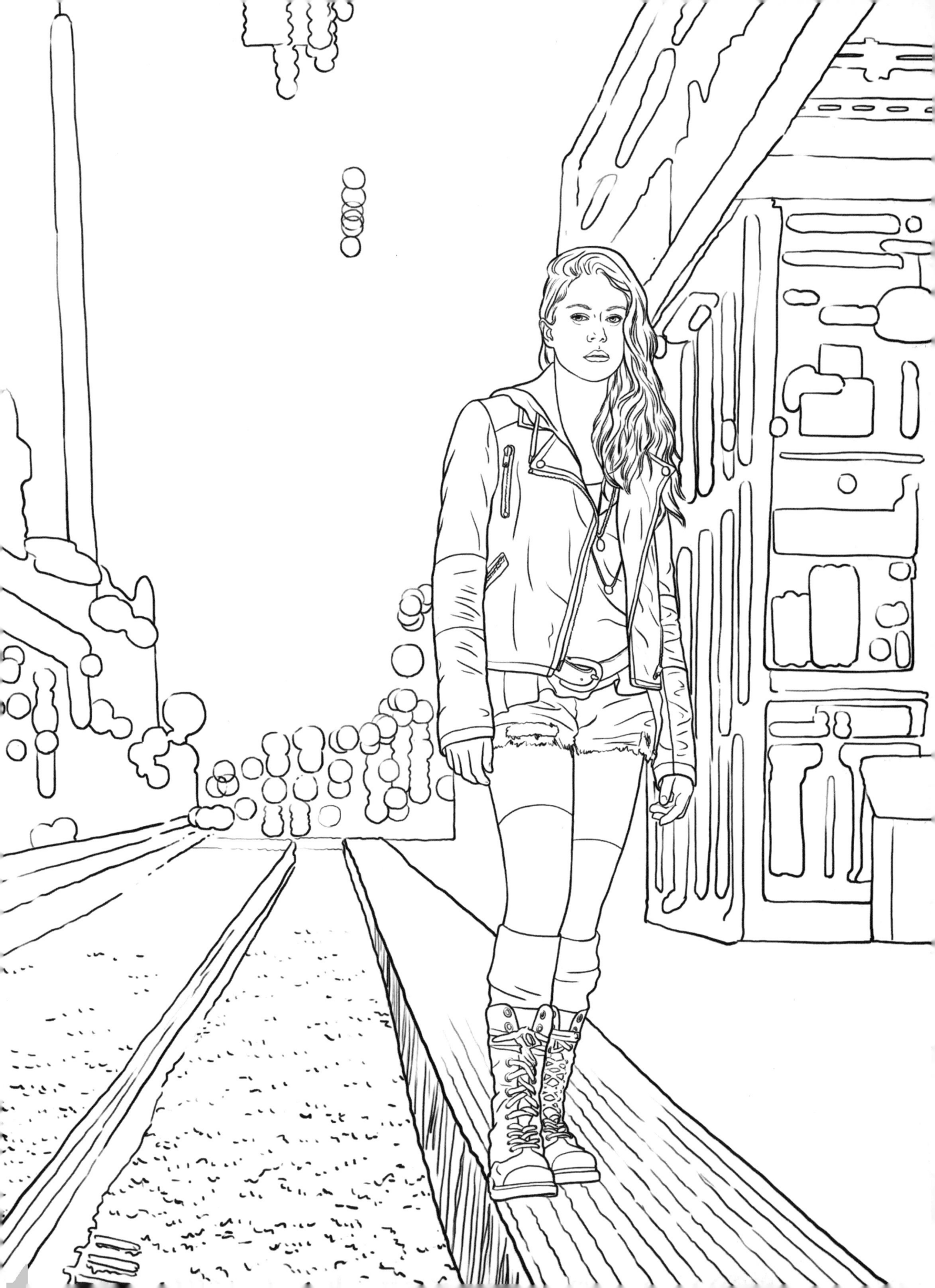

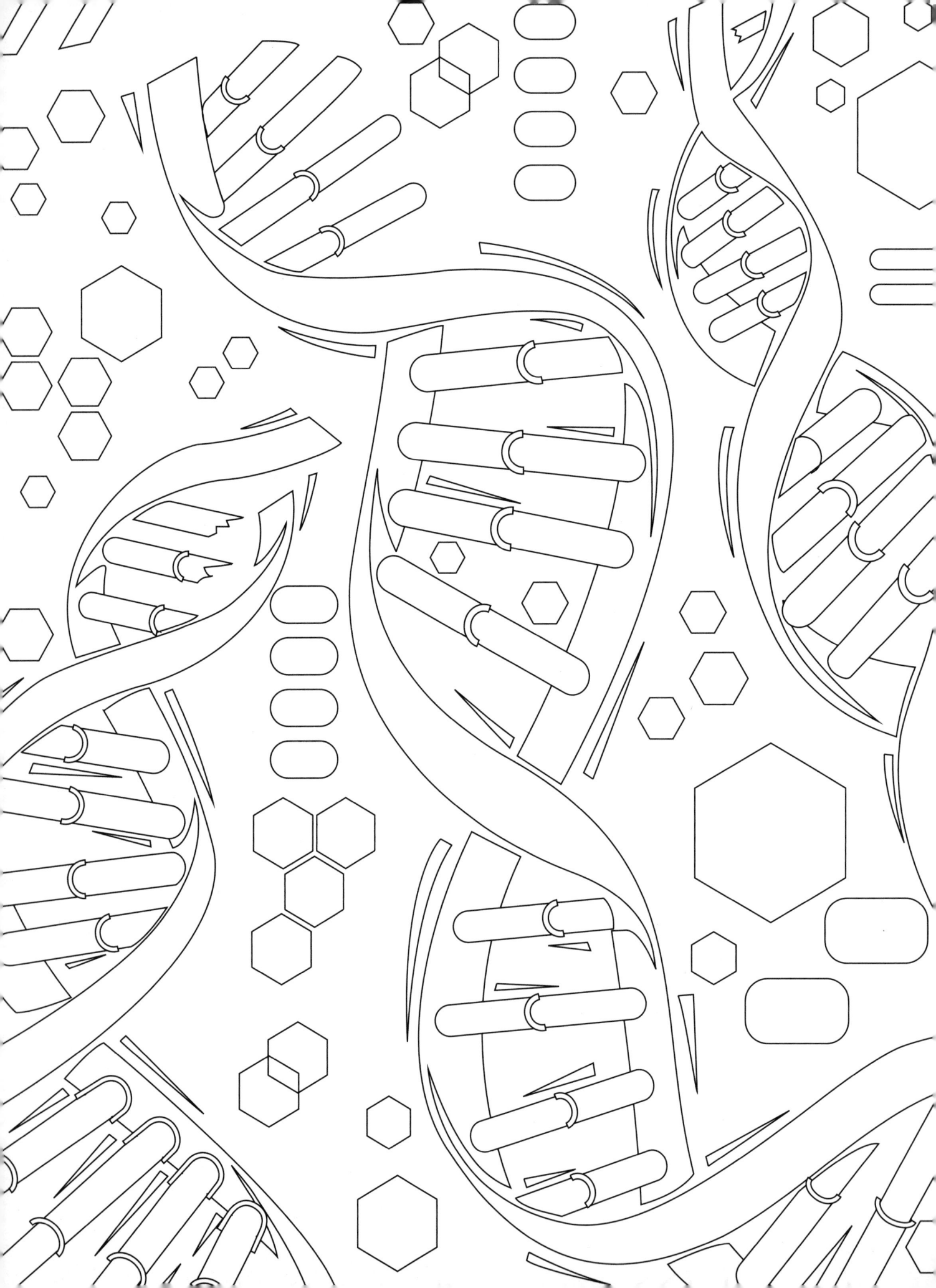

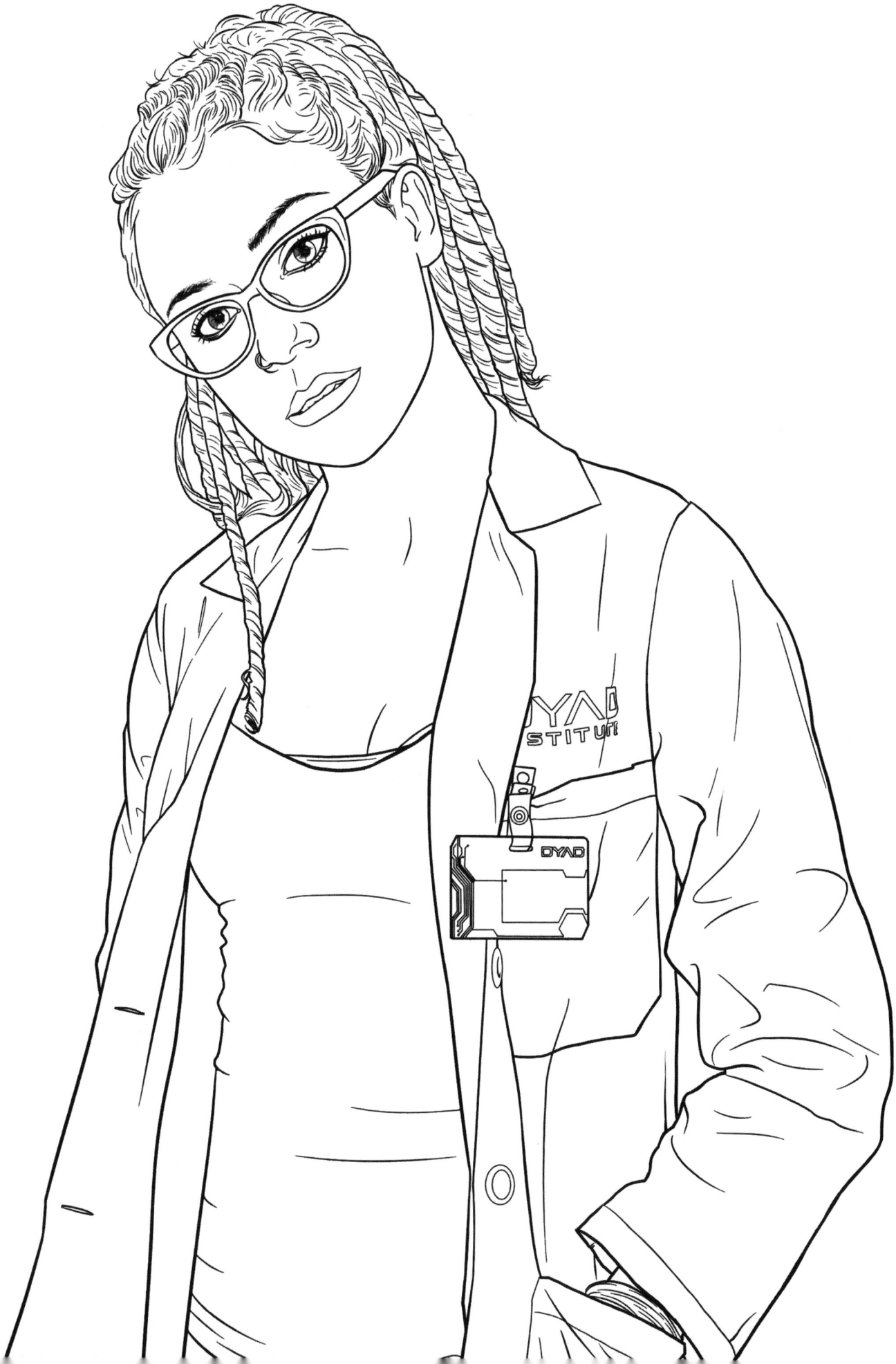
DYAD

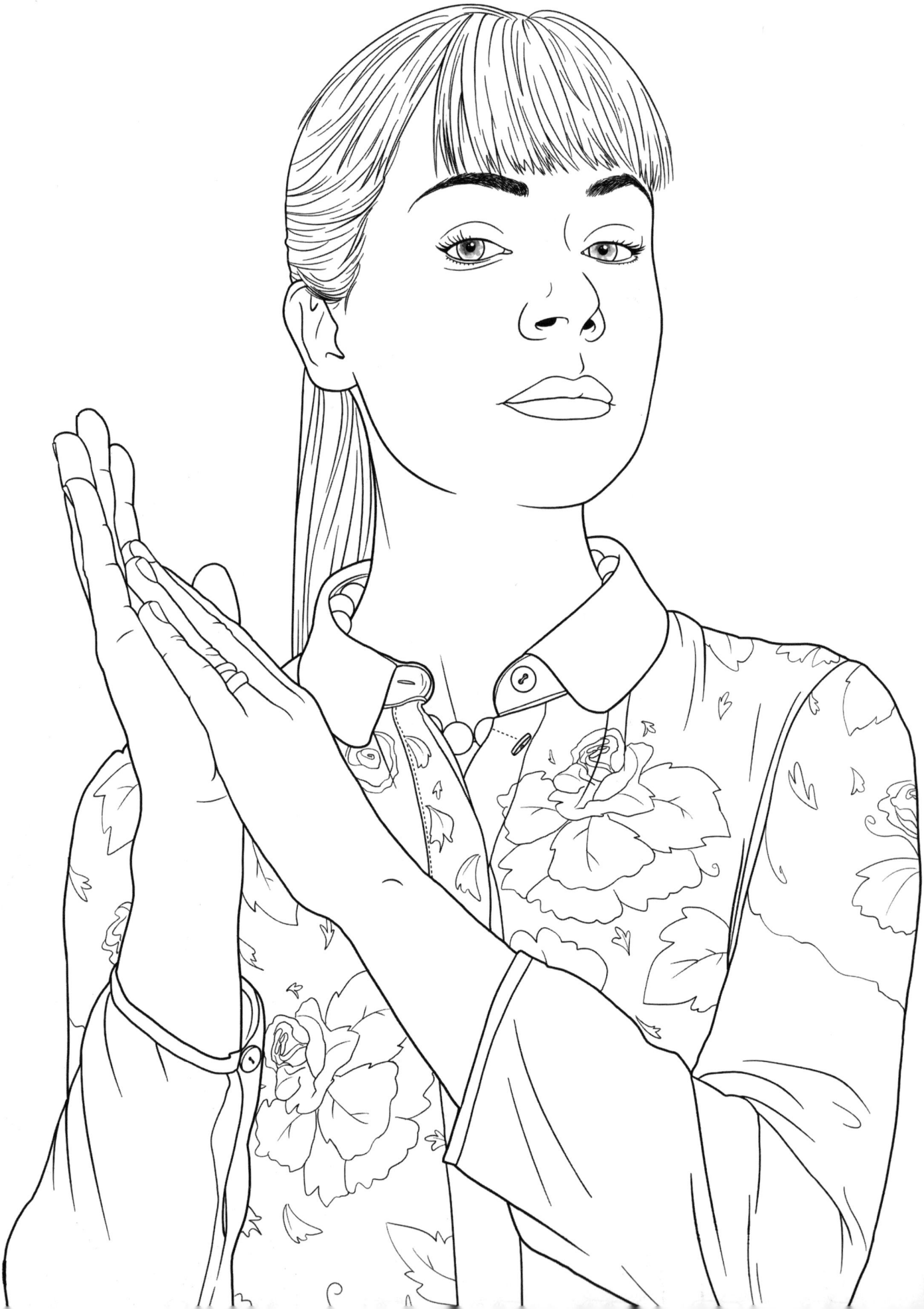

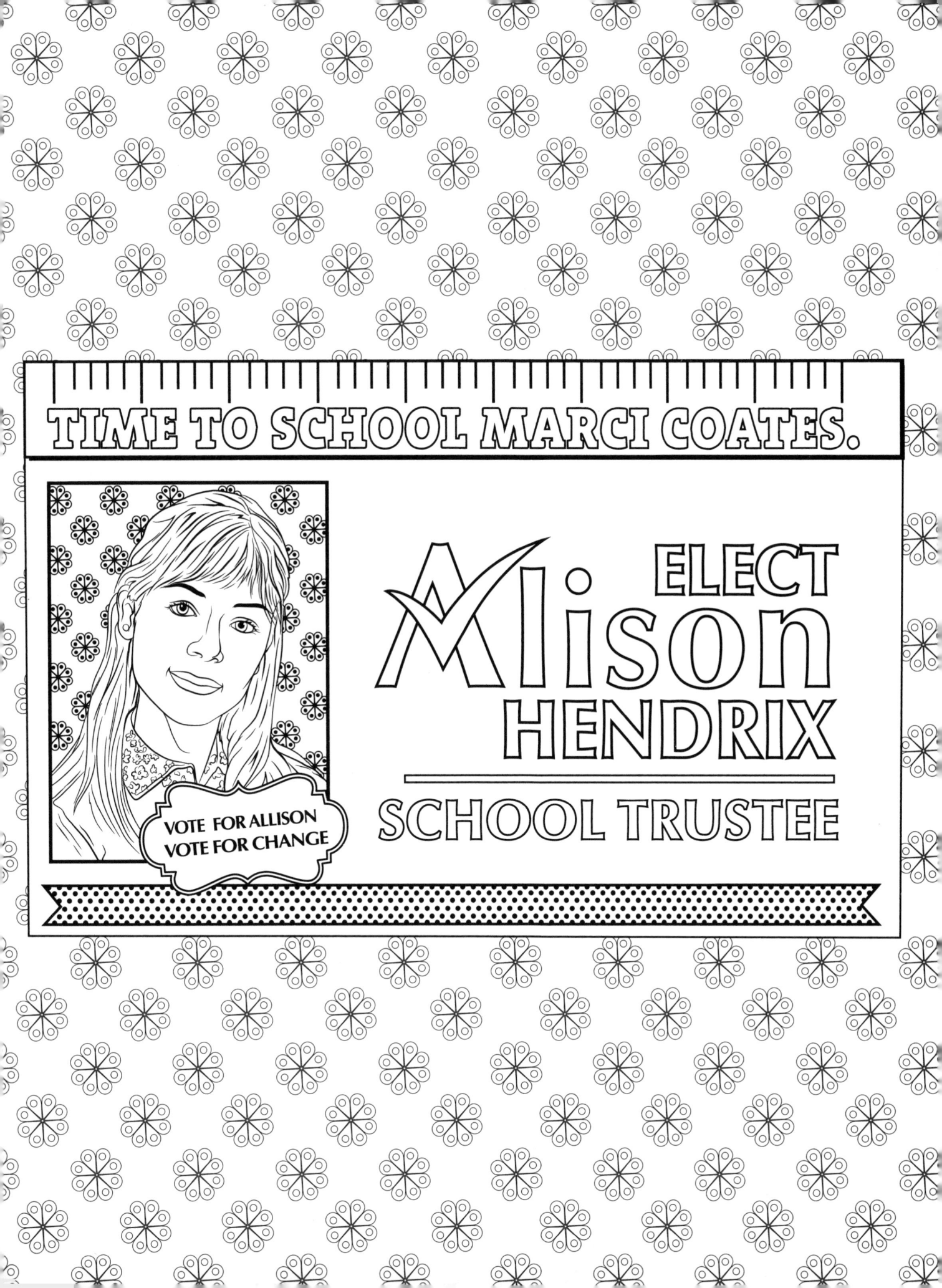
TIME TO SCHOOL MARCI COATES.
VOTE FOR ALLISON
VOTE FOR CHANGE
ELECT
Alison
HENDRIX
SCHOOL TRUSTEE

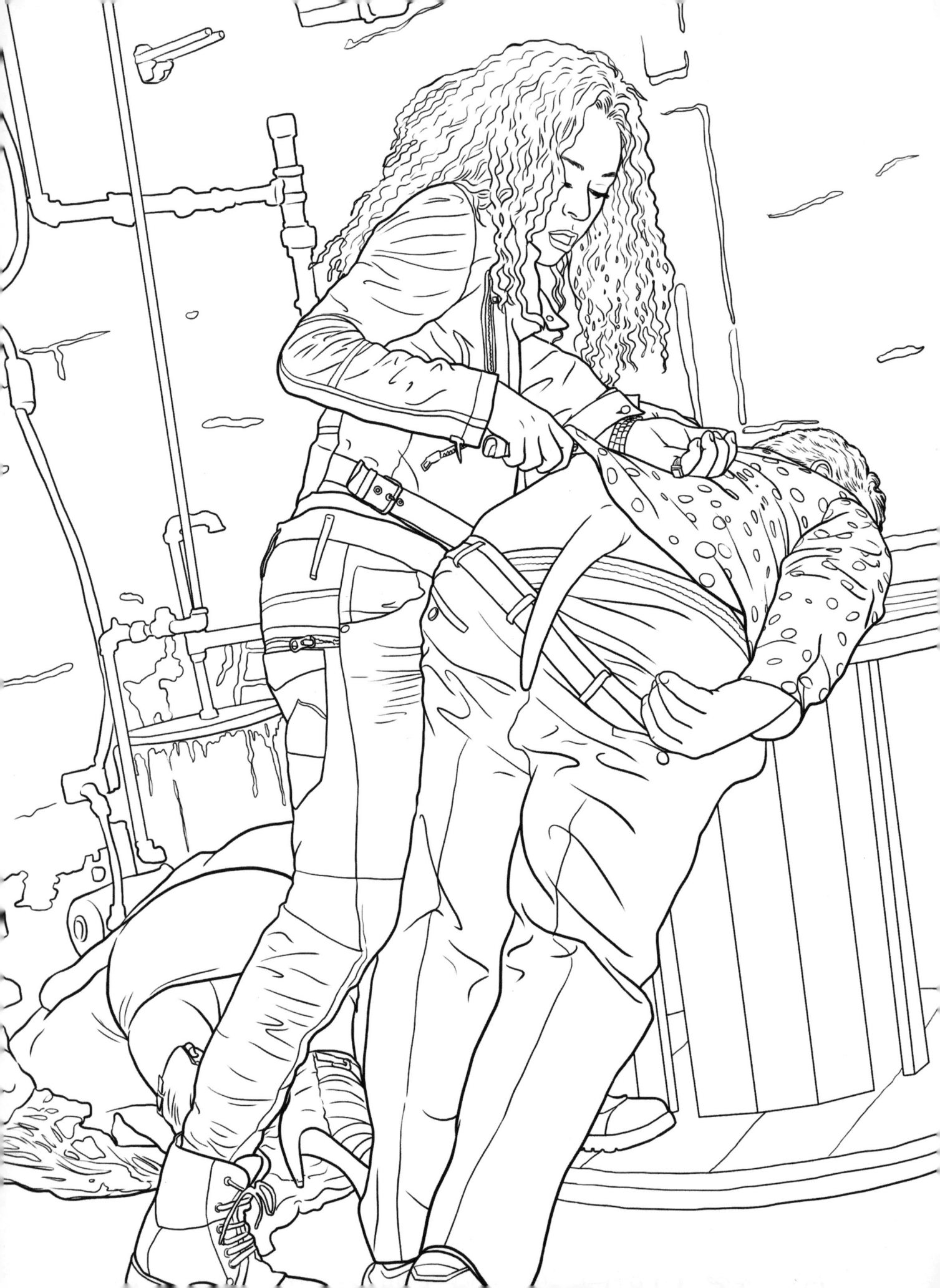

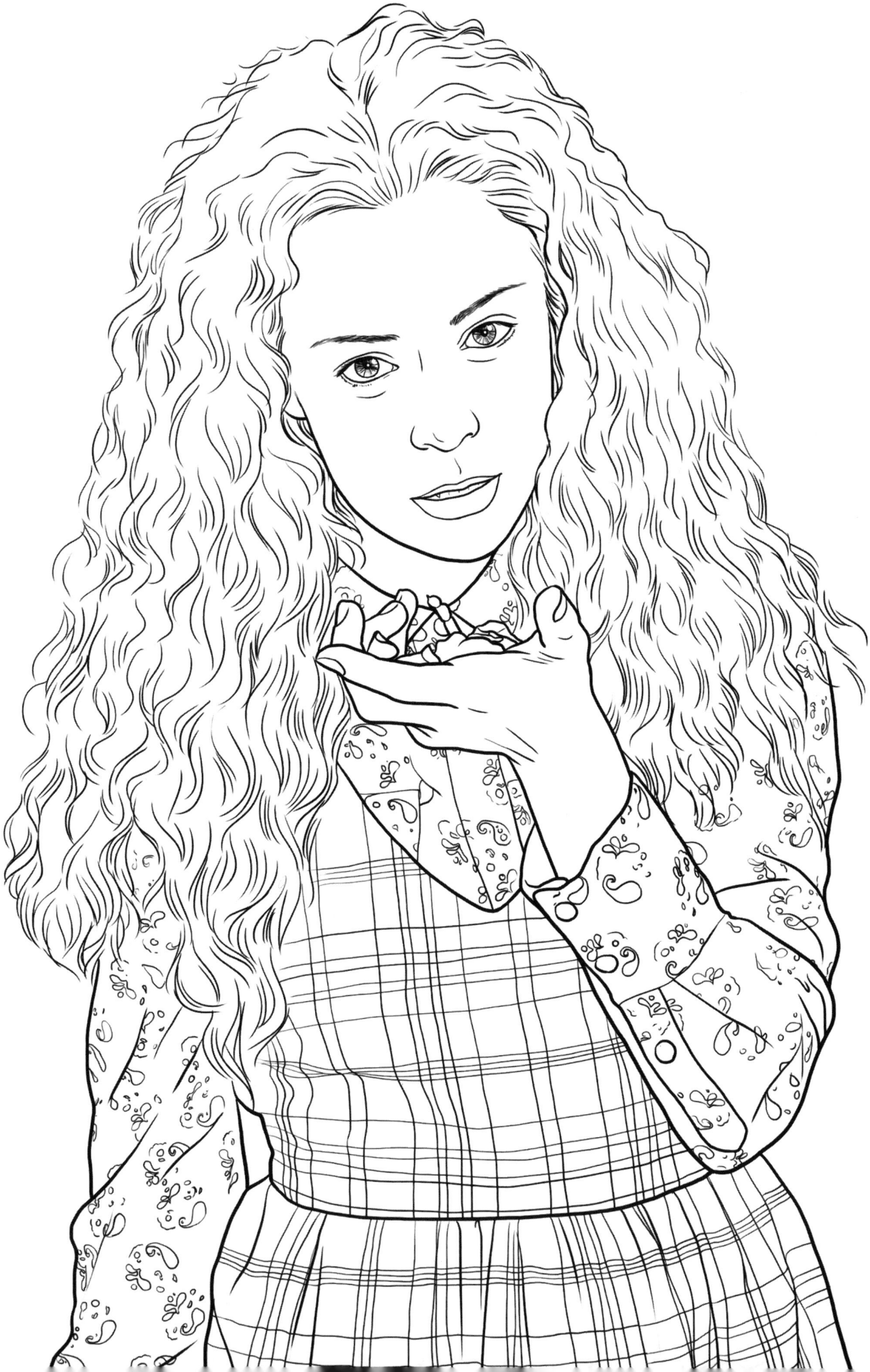

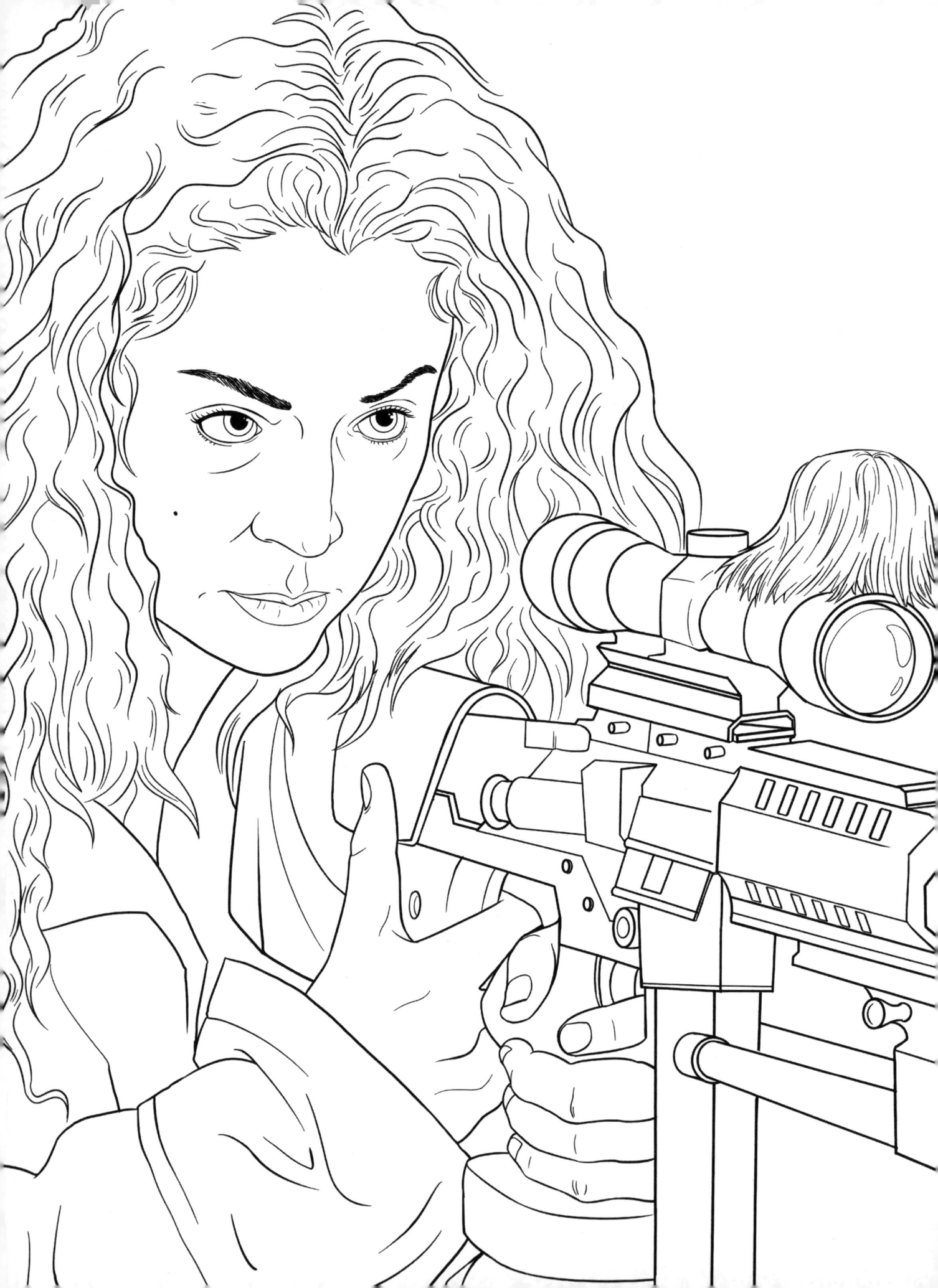

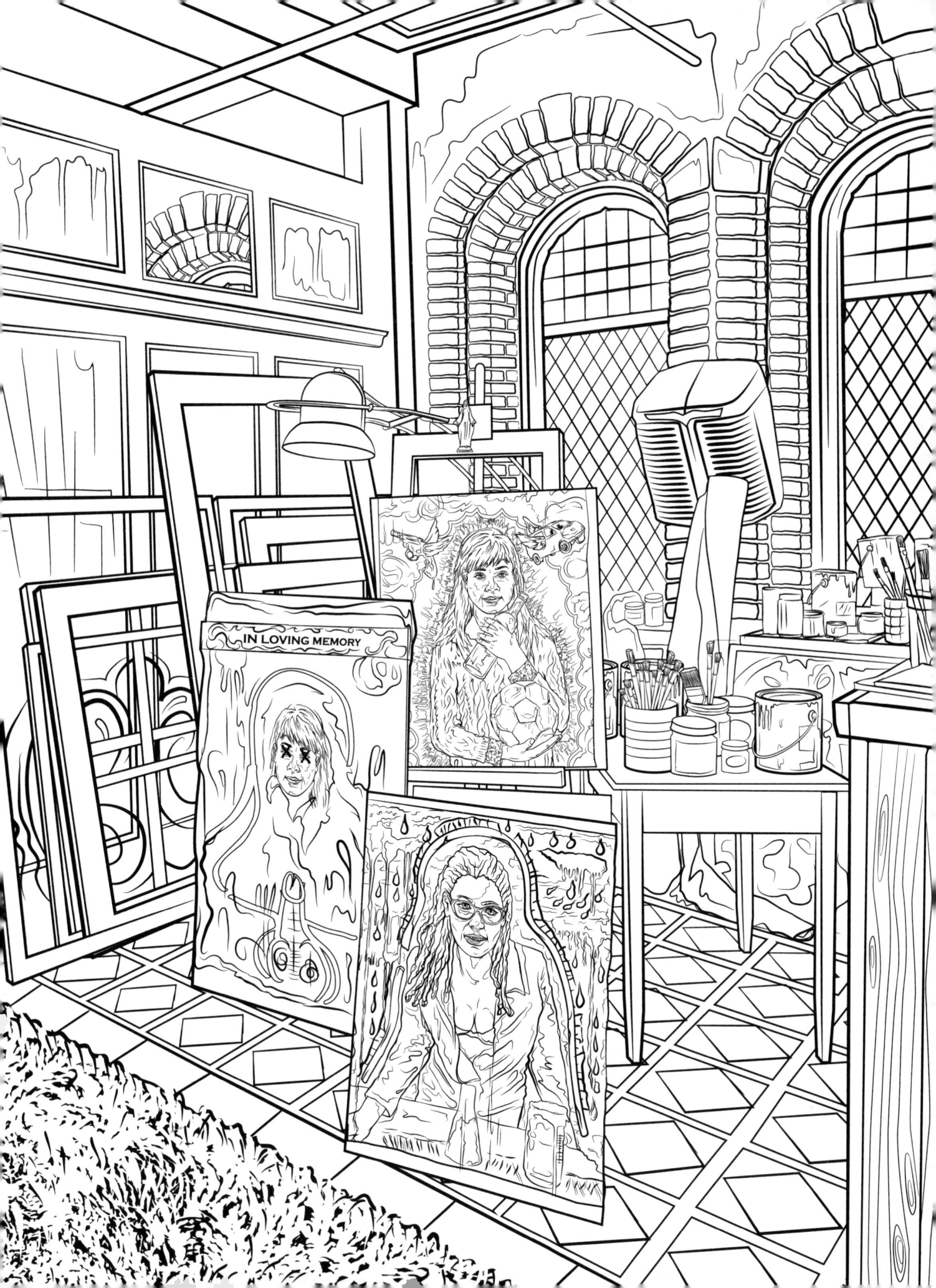
IN LOVING MEMORY

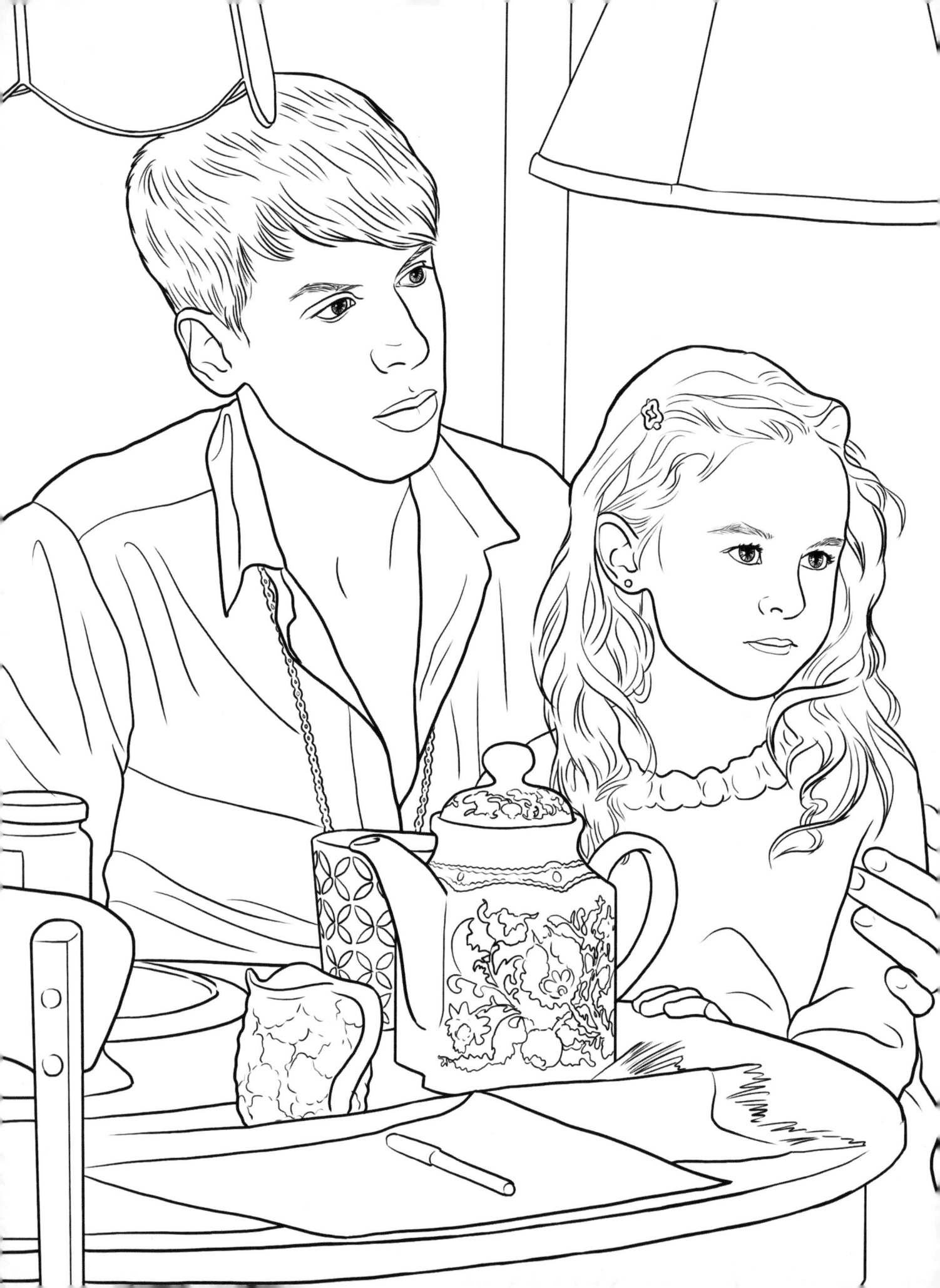

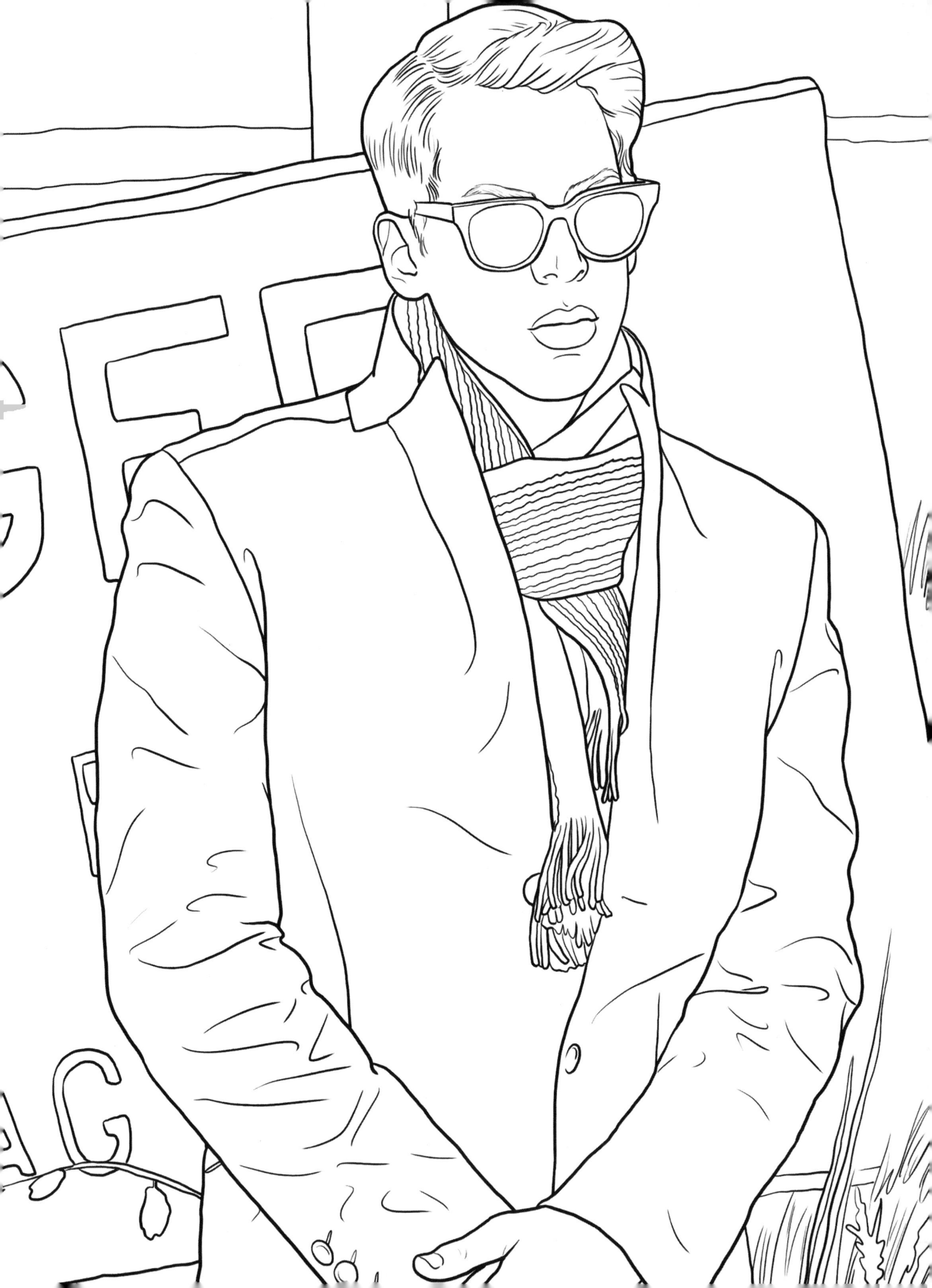

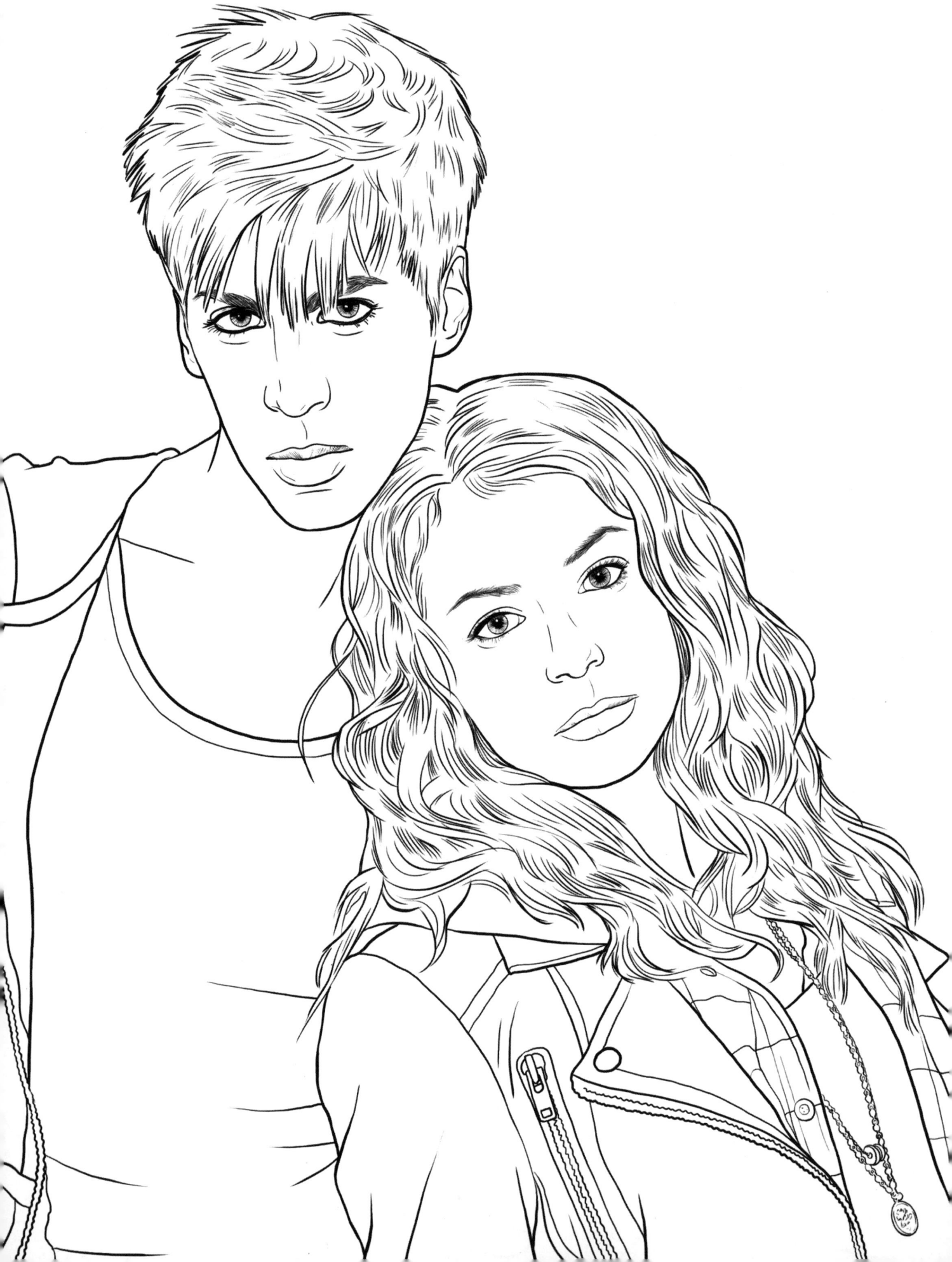

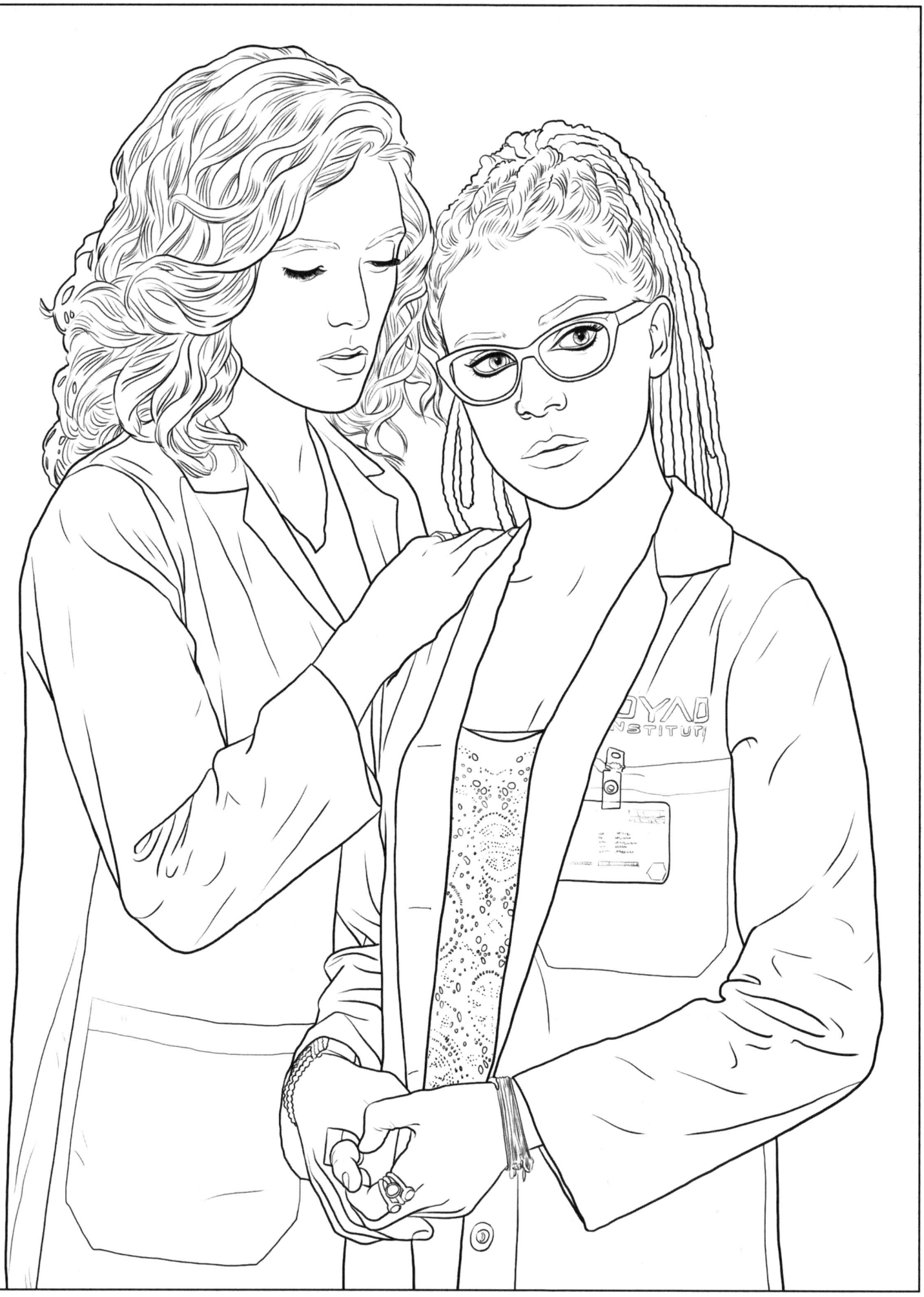

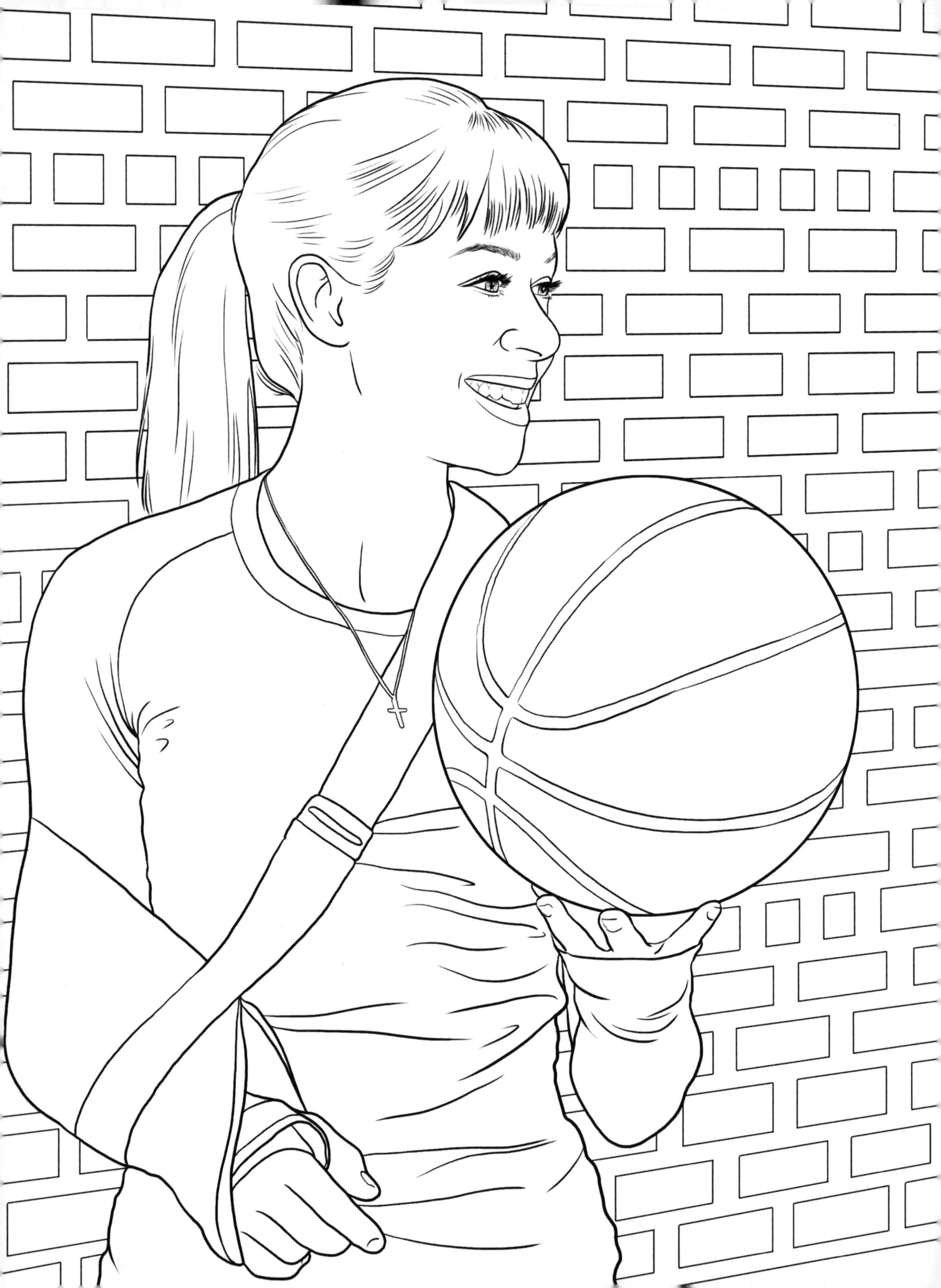

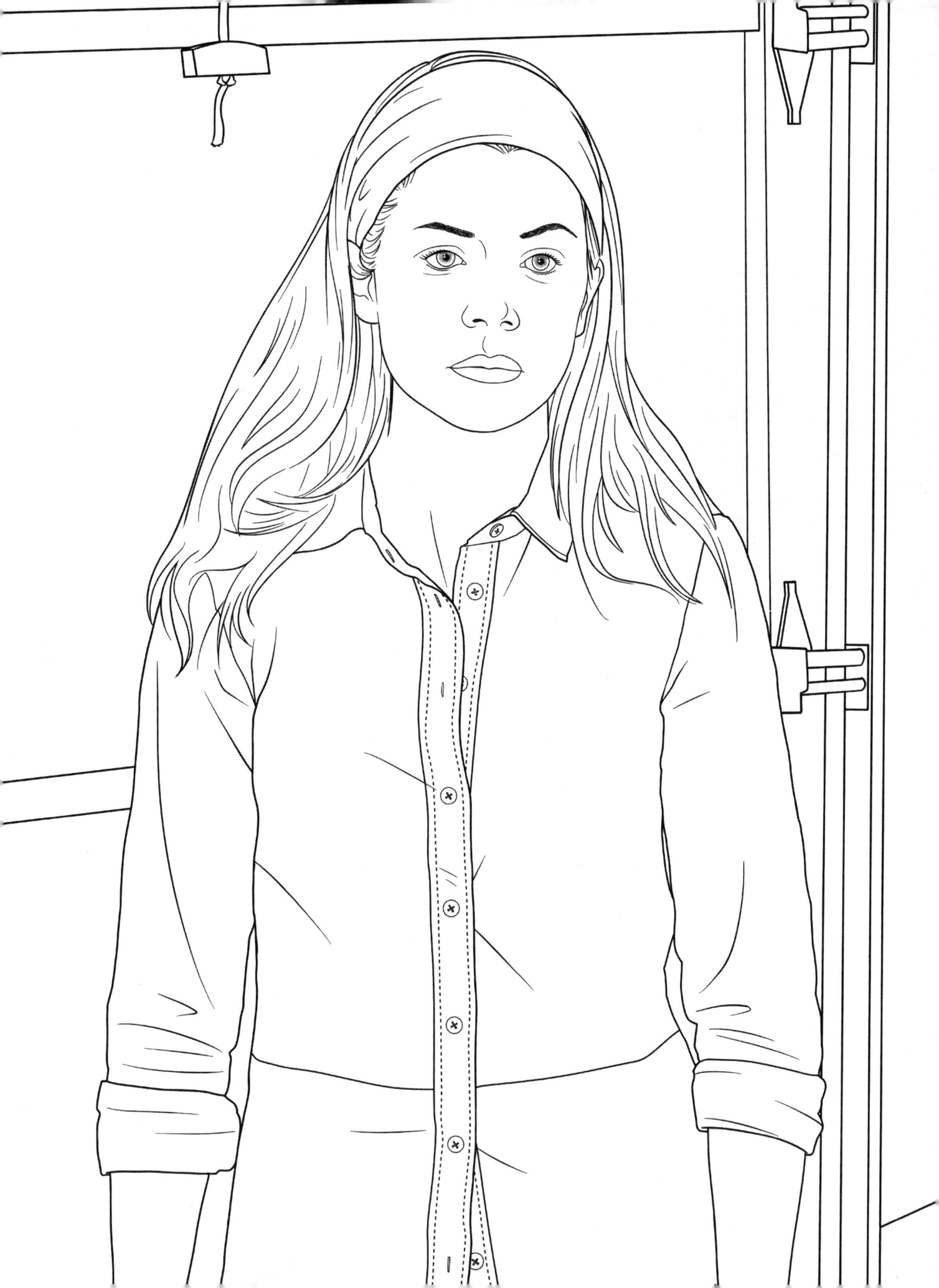

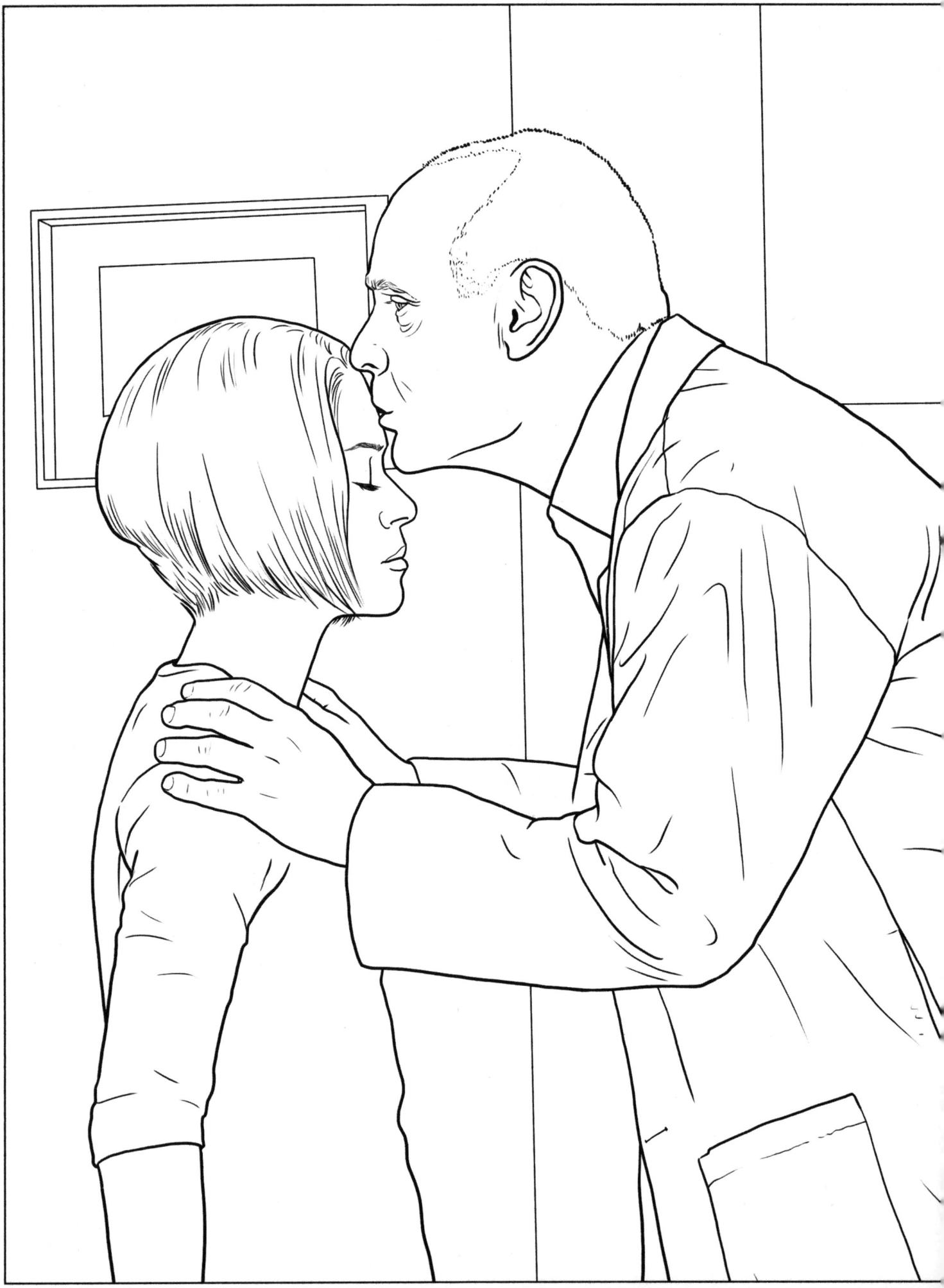

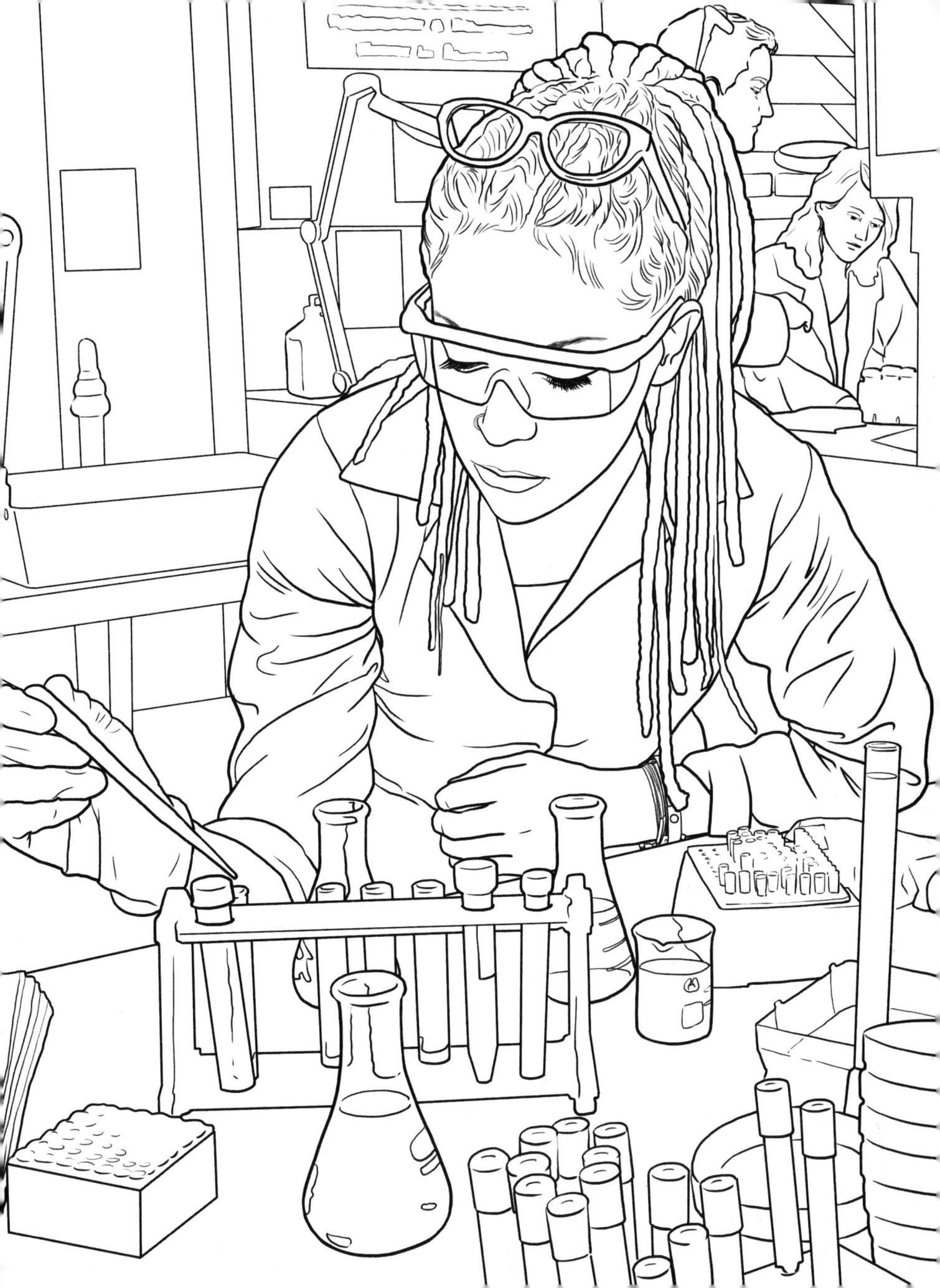

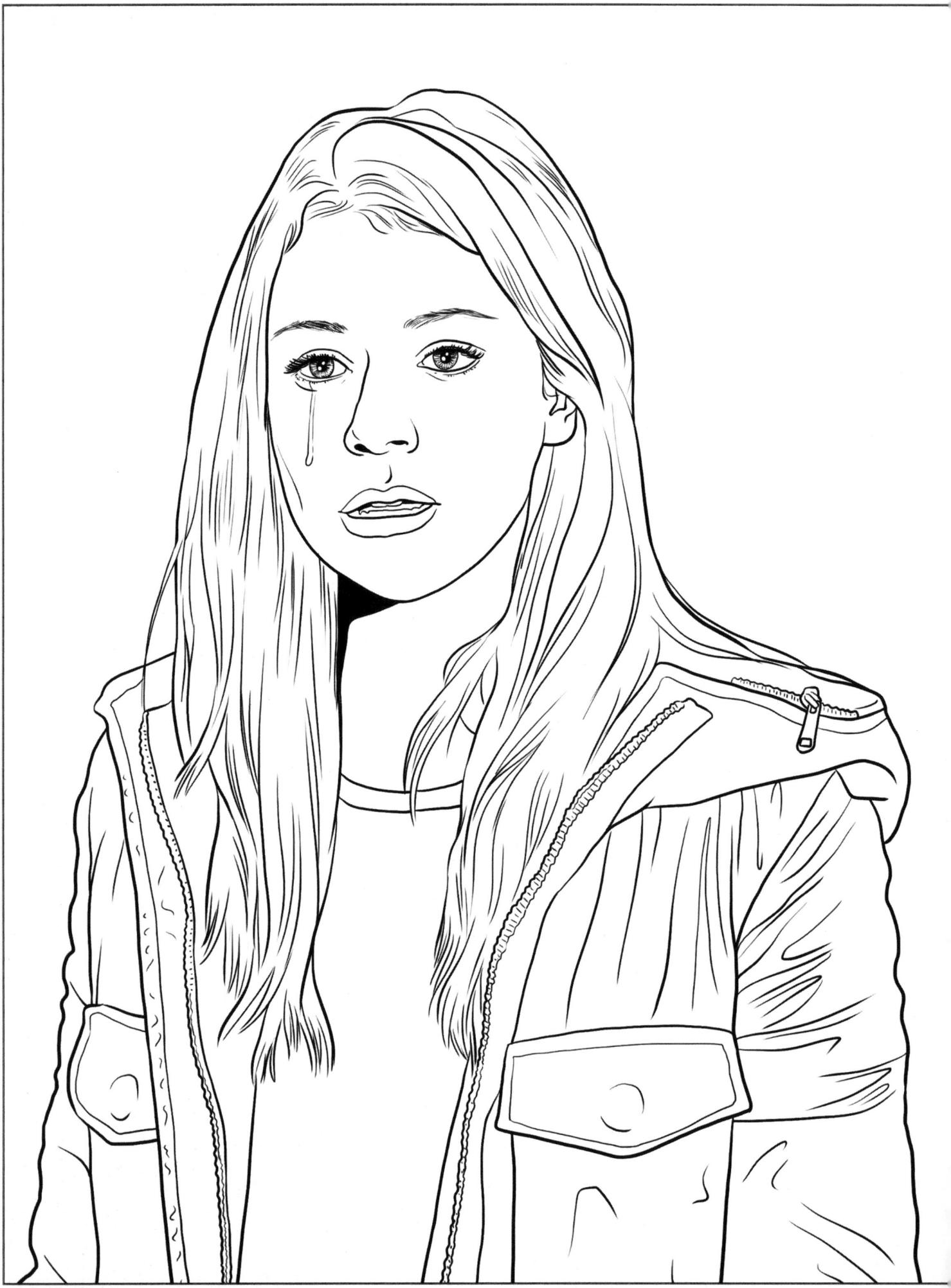

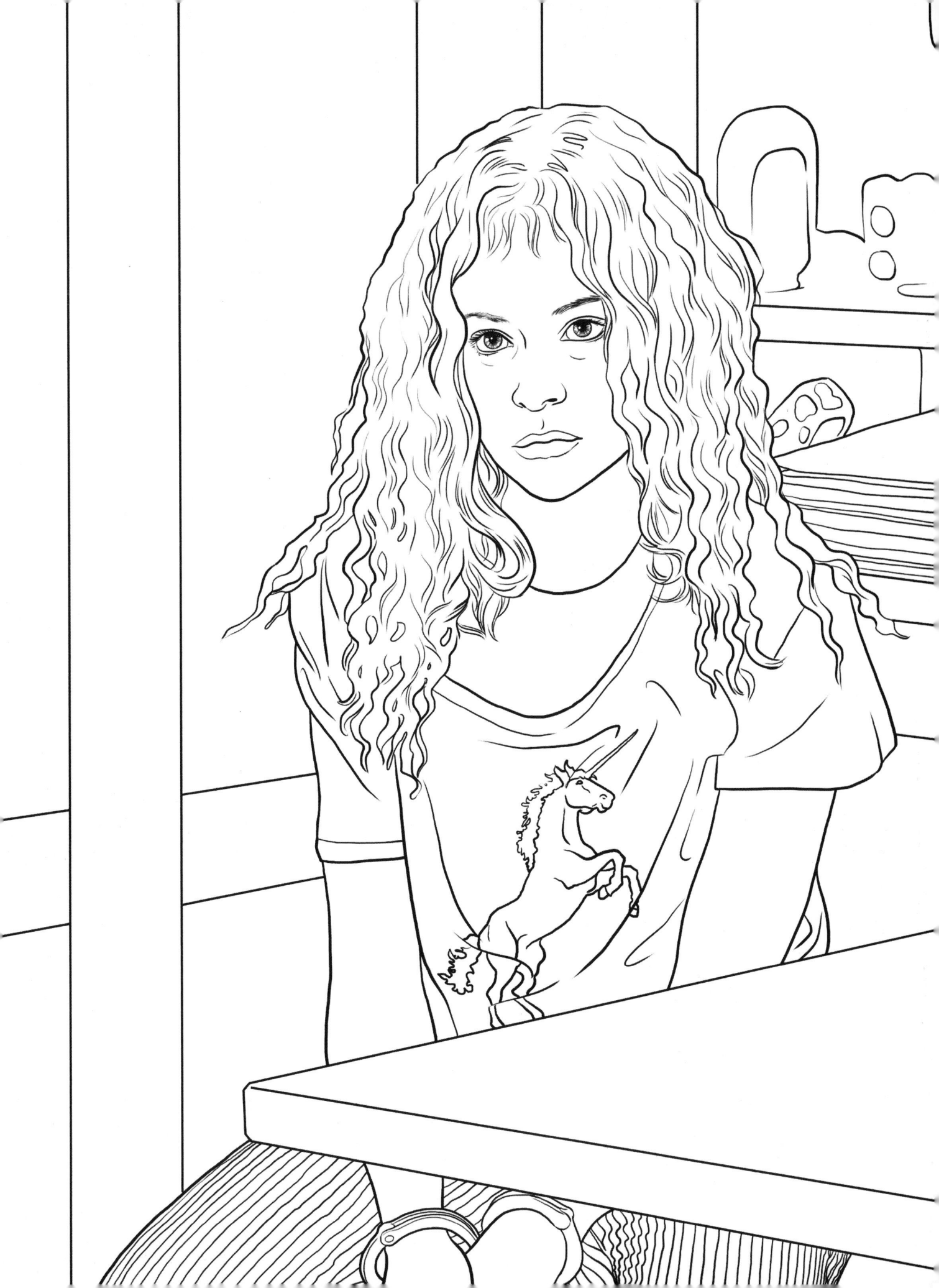

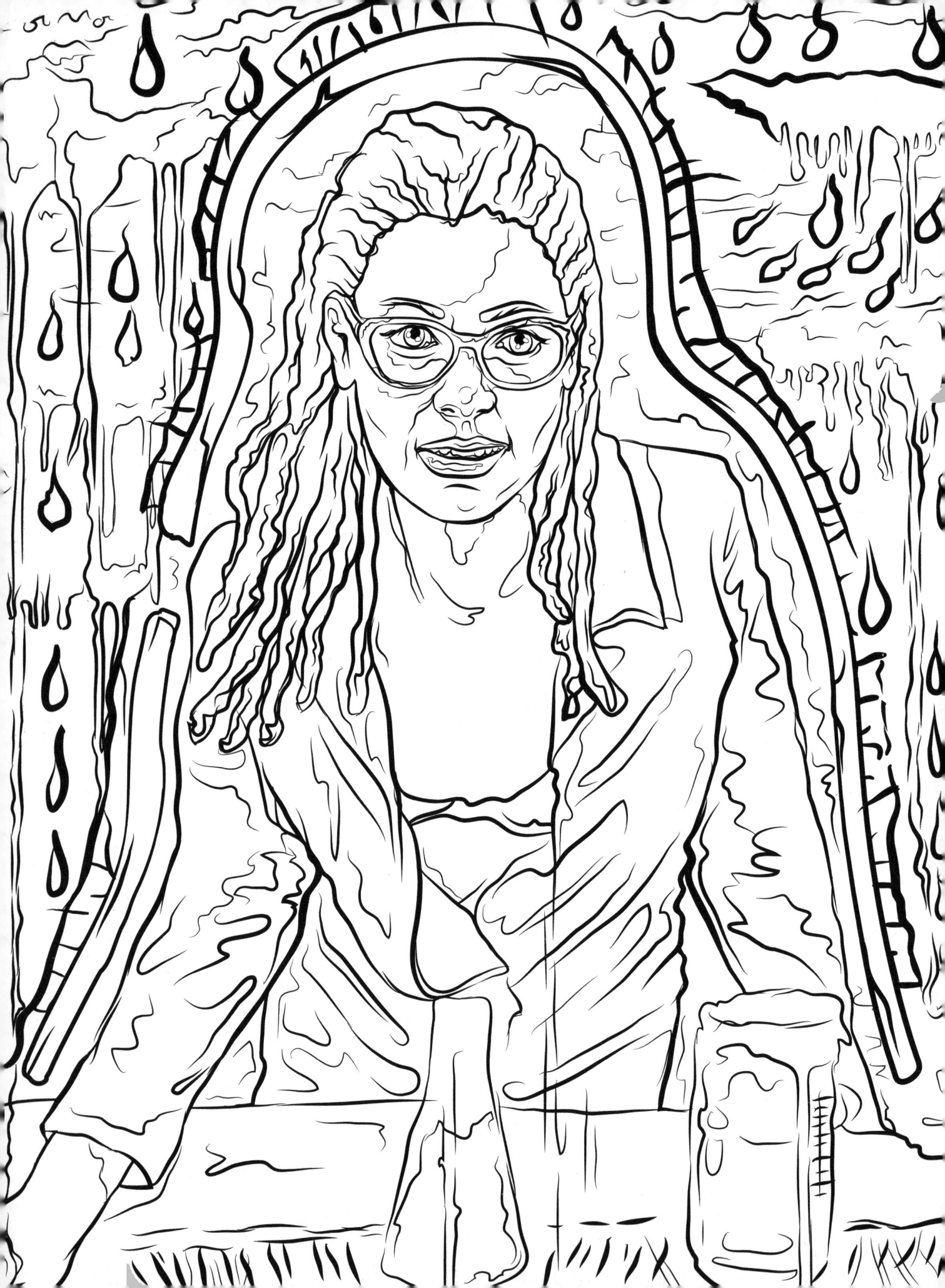

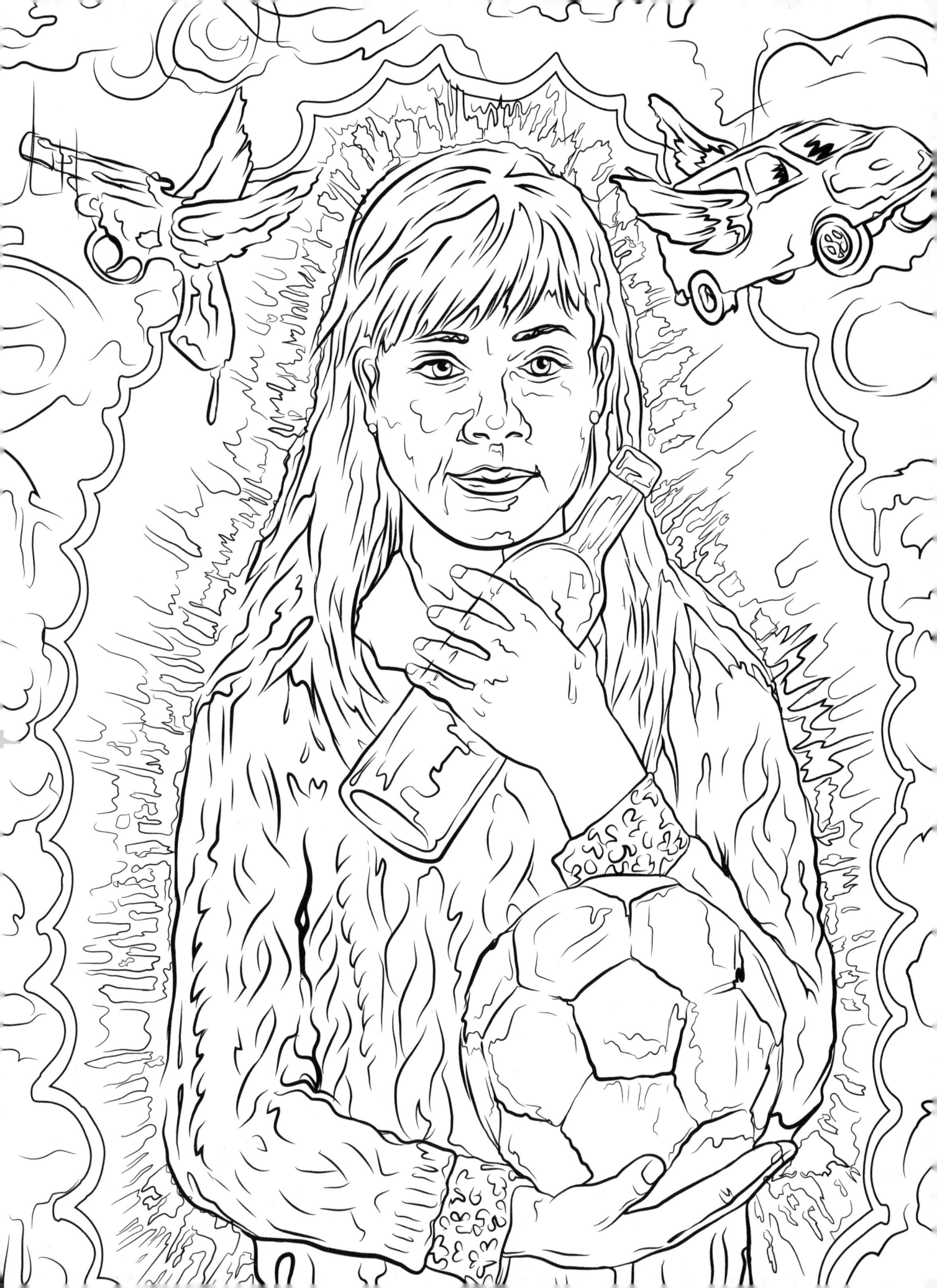

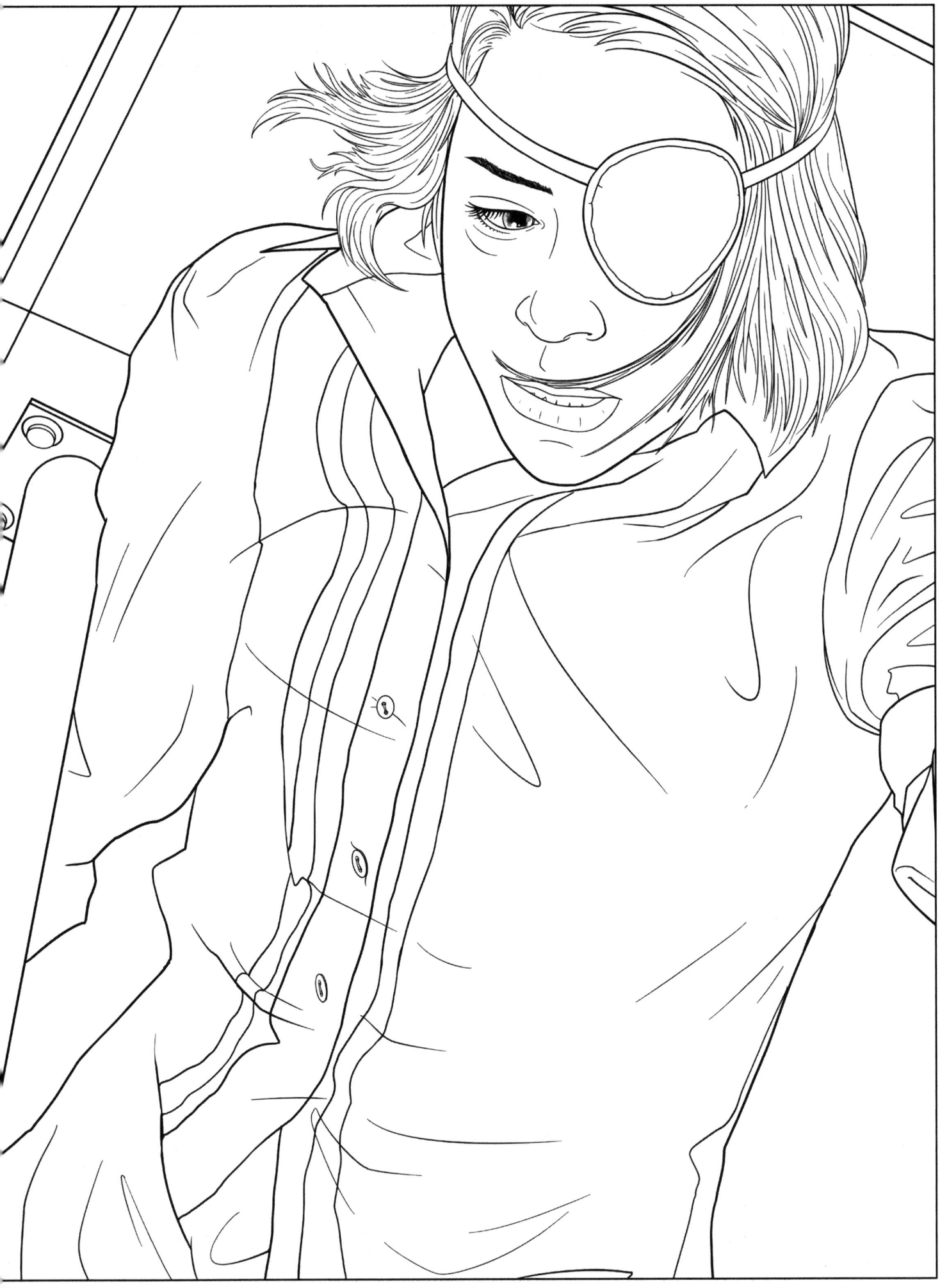

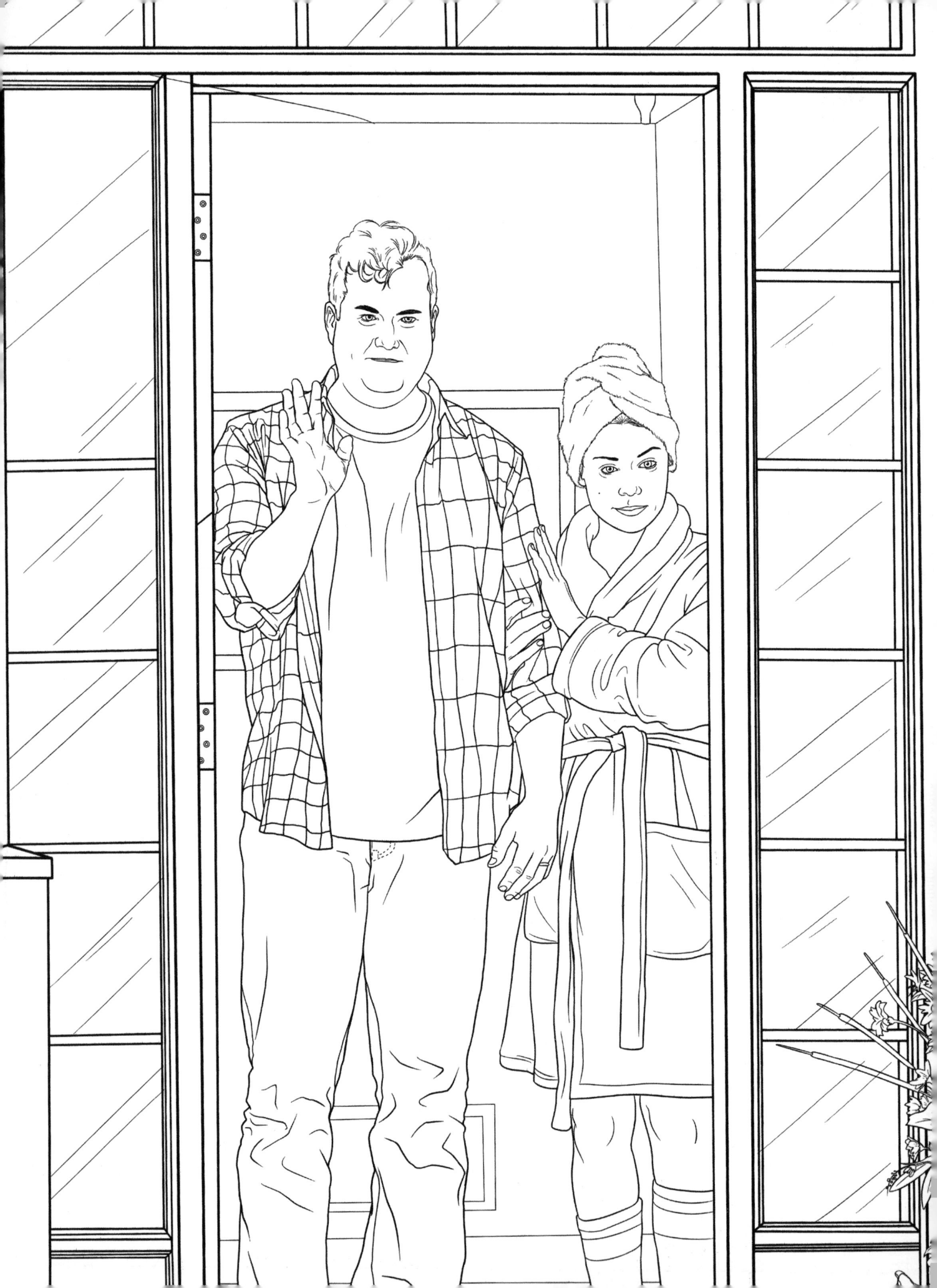

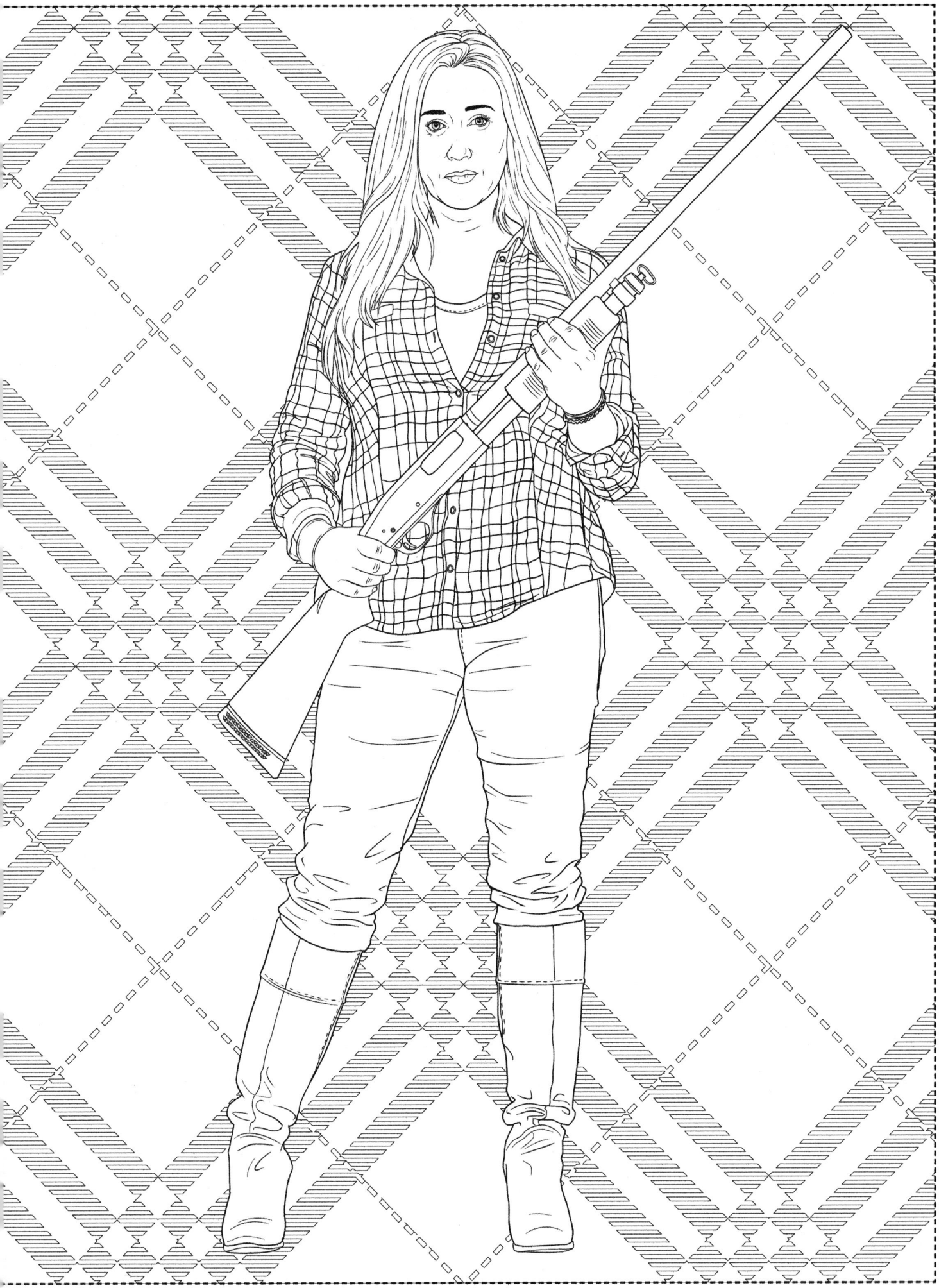

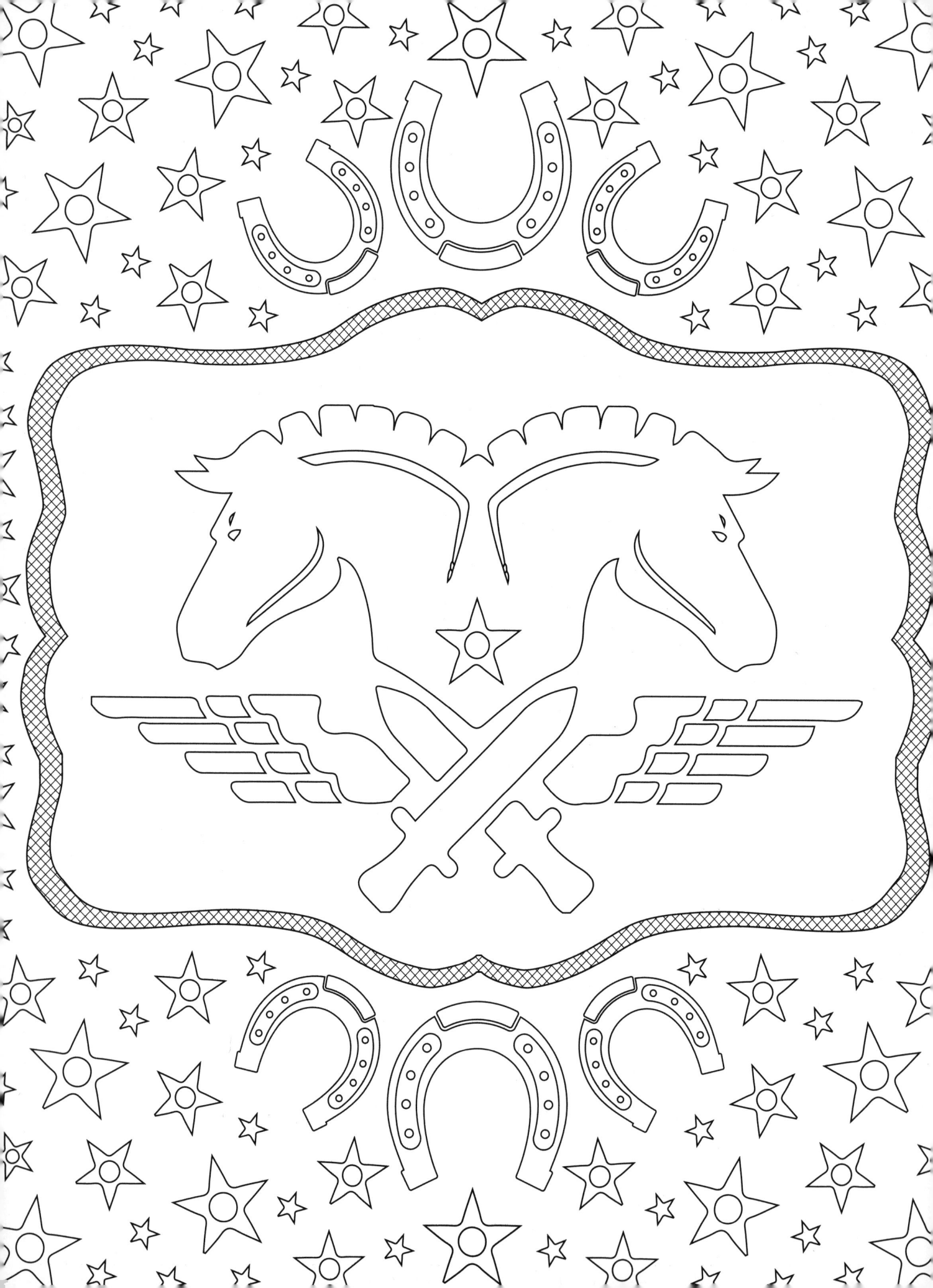

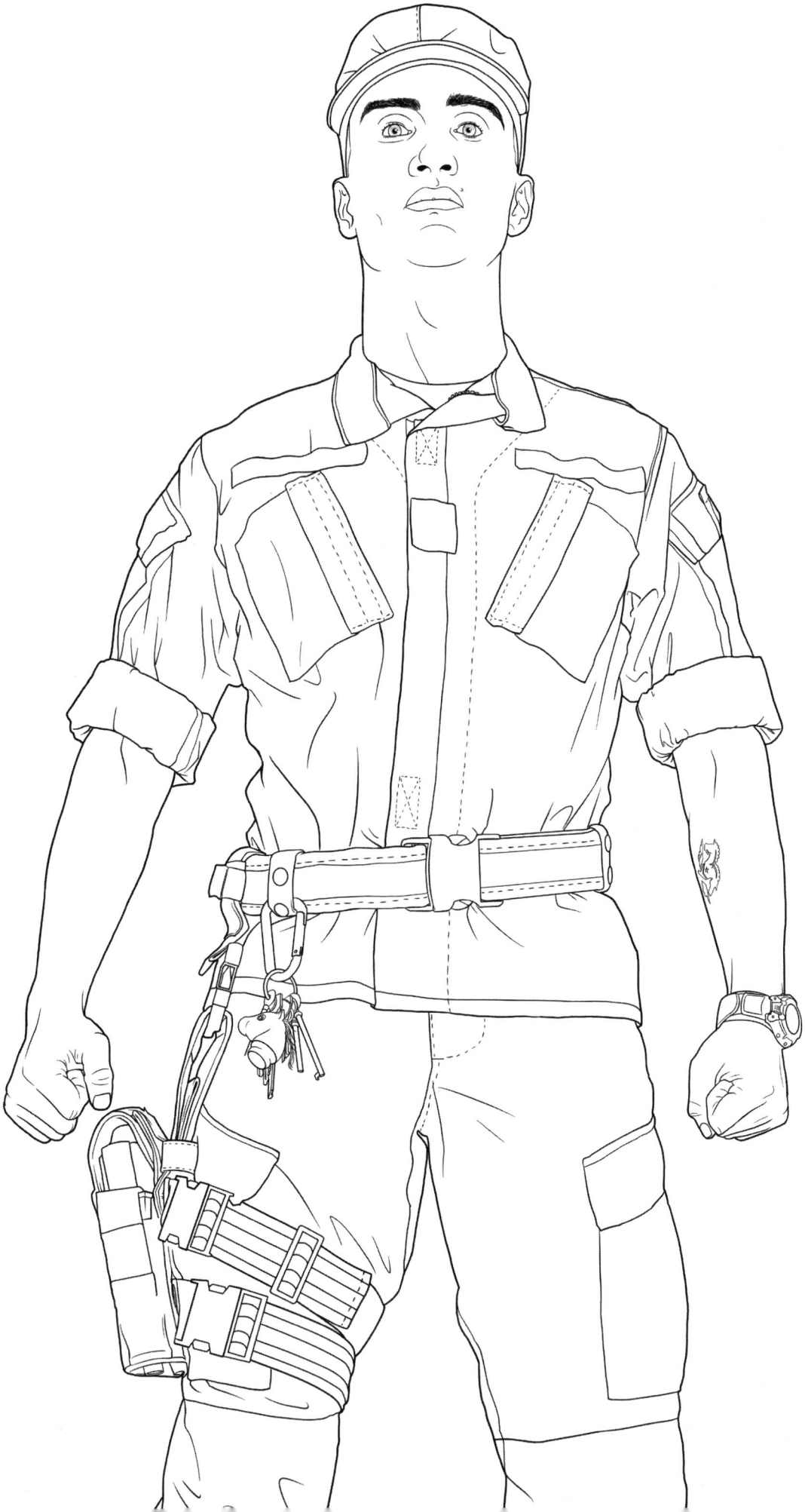

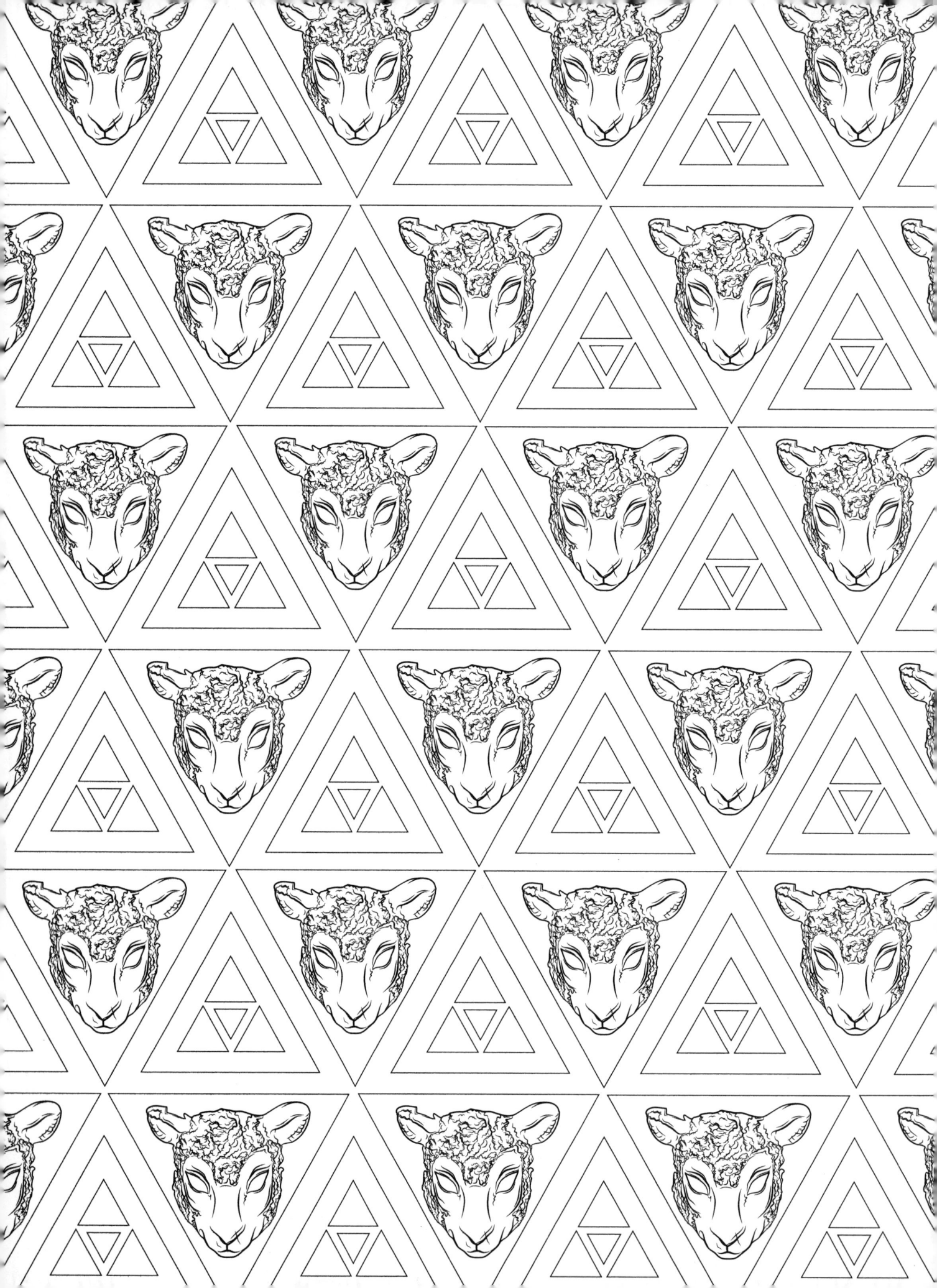

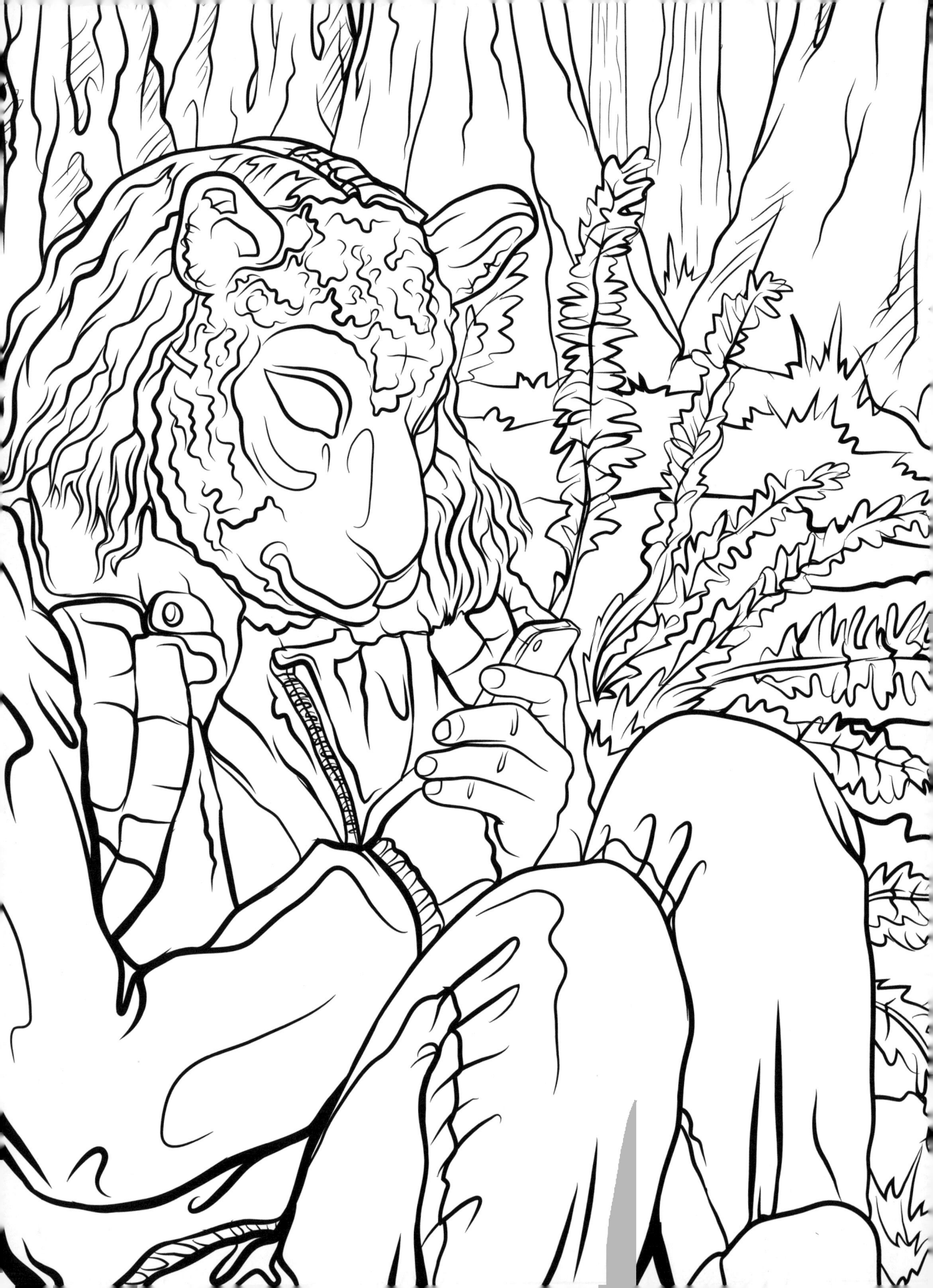

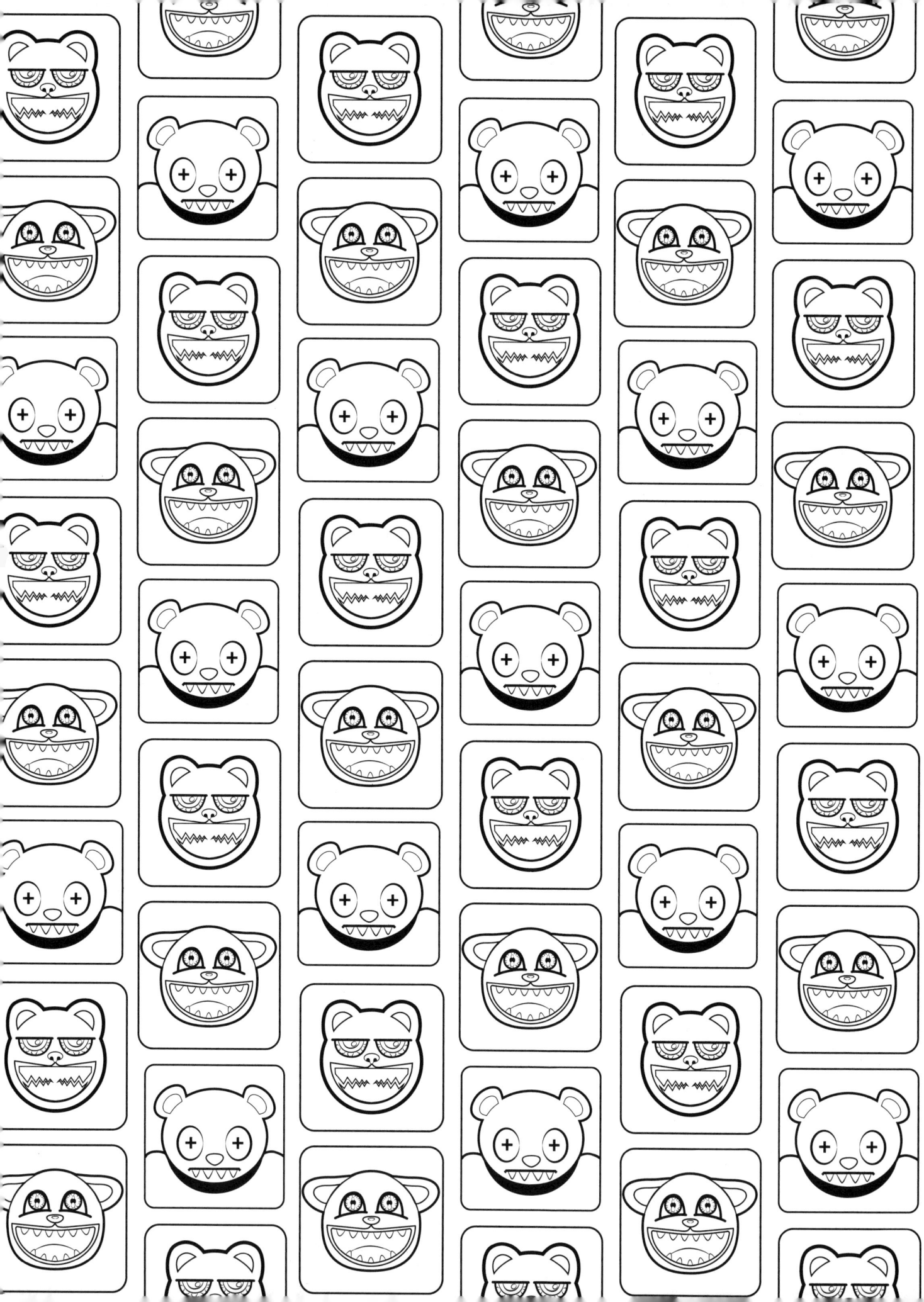

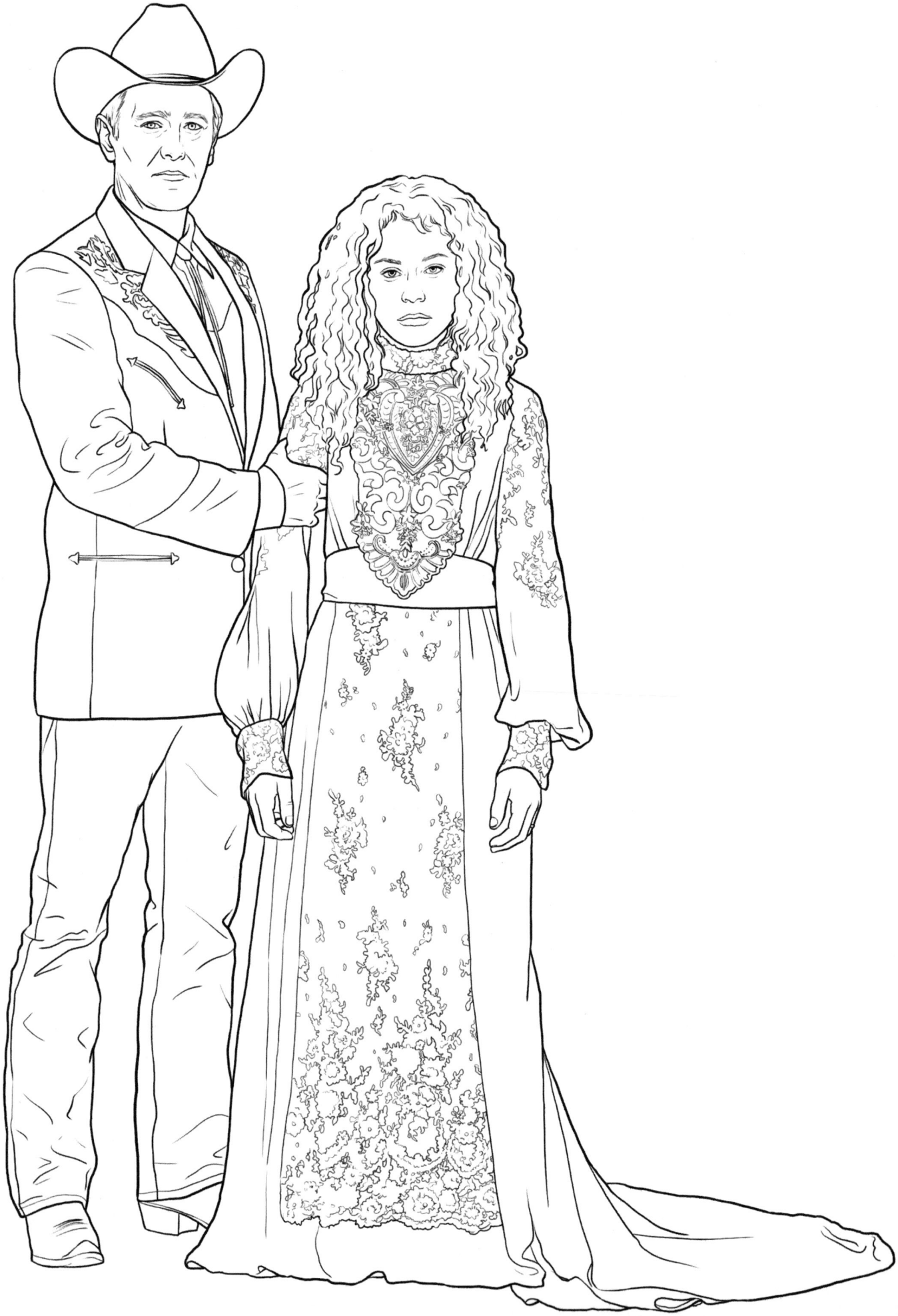

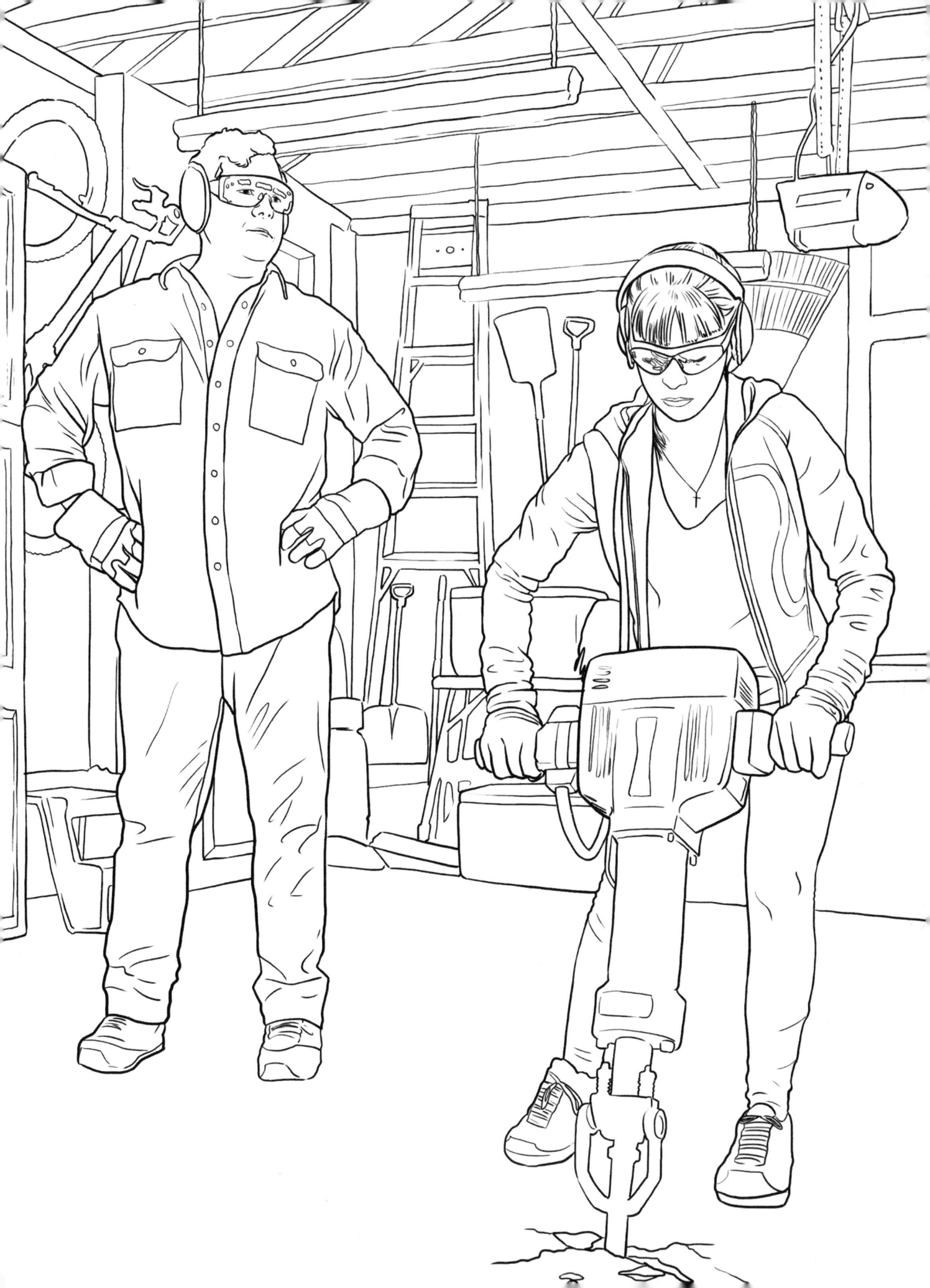

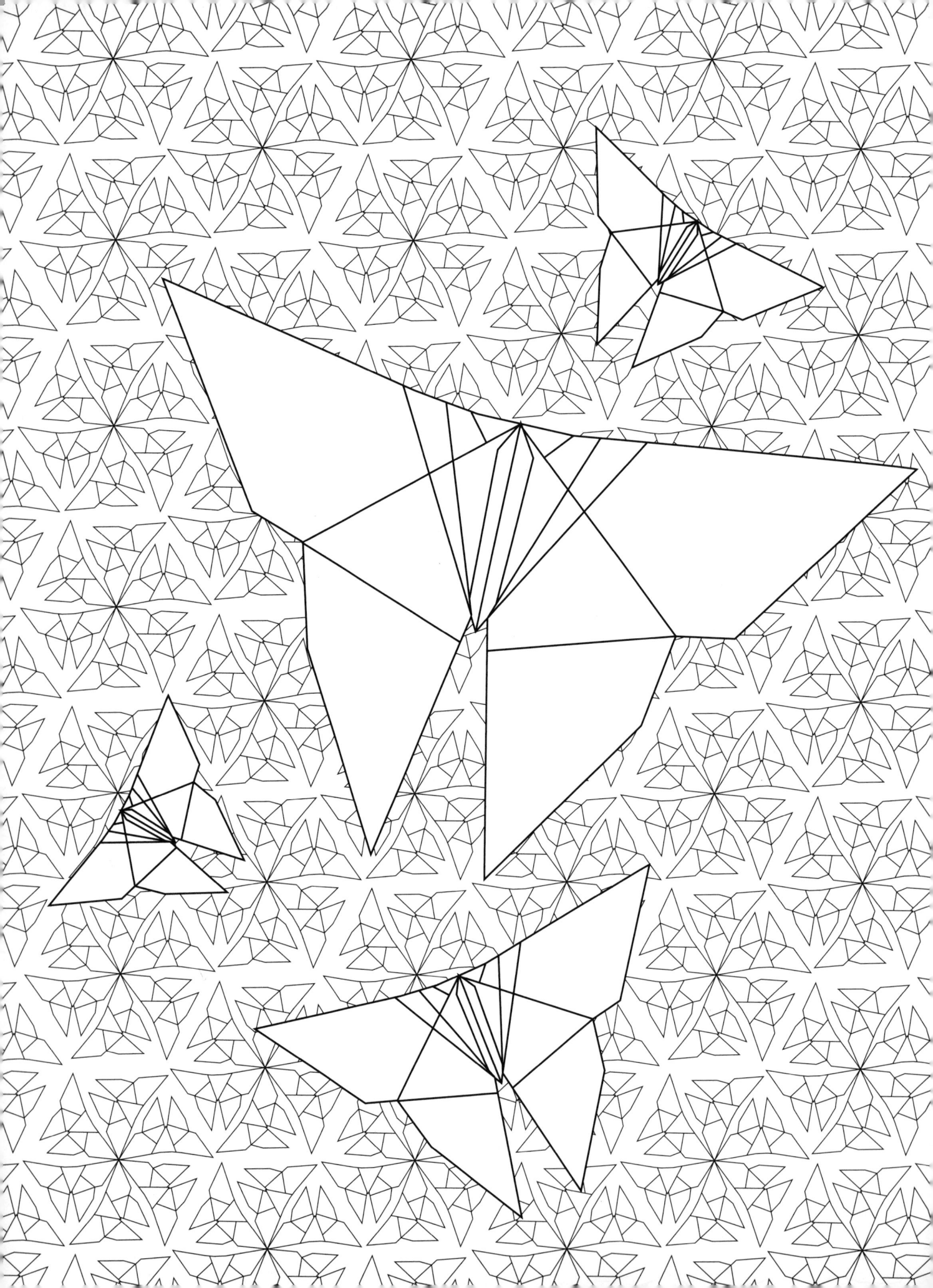

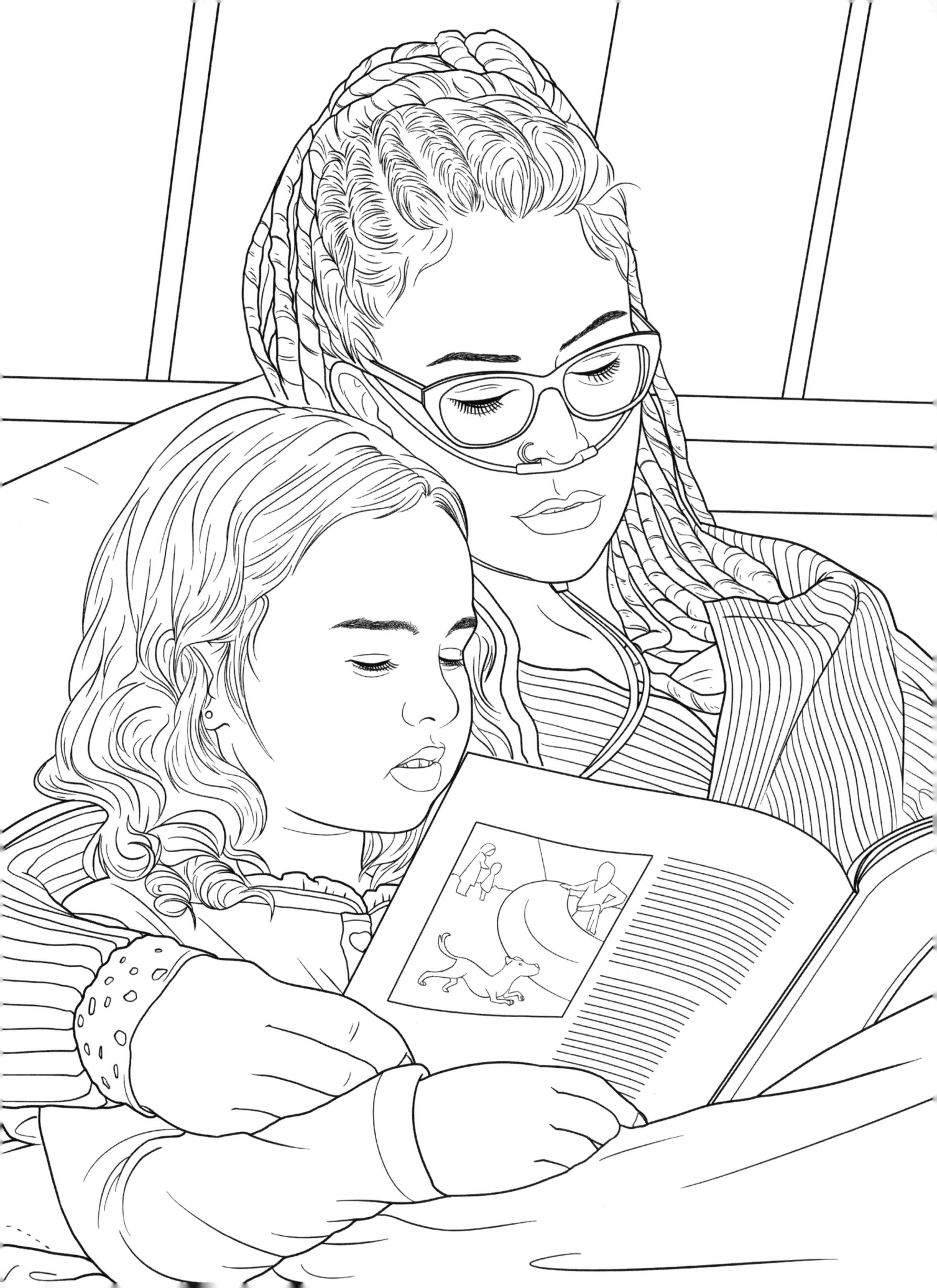

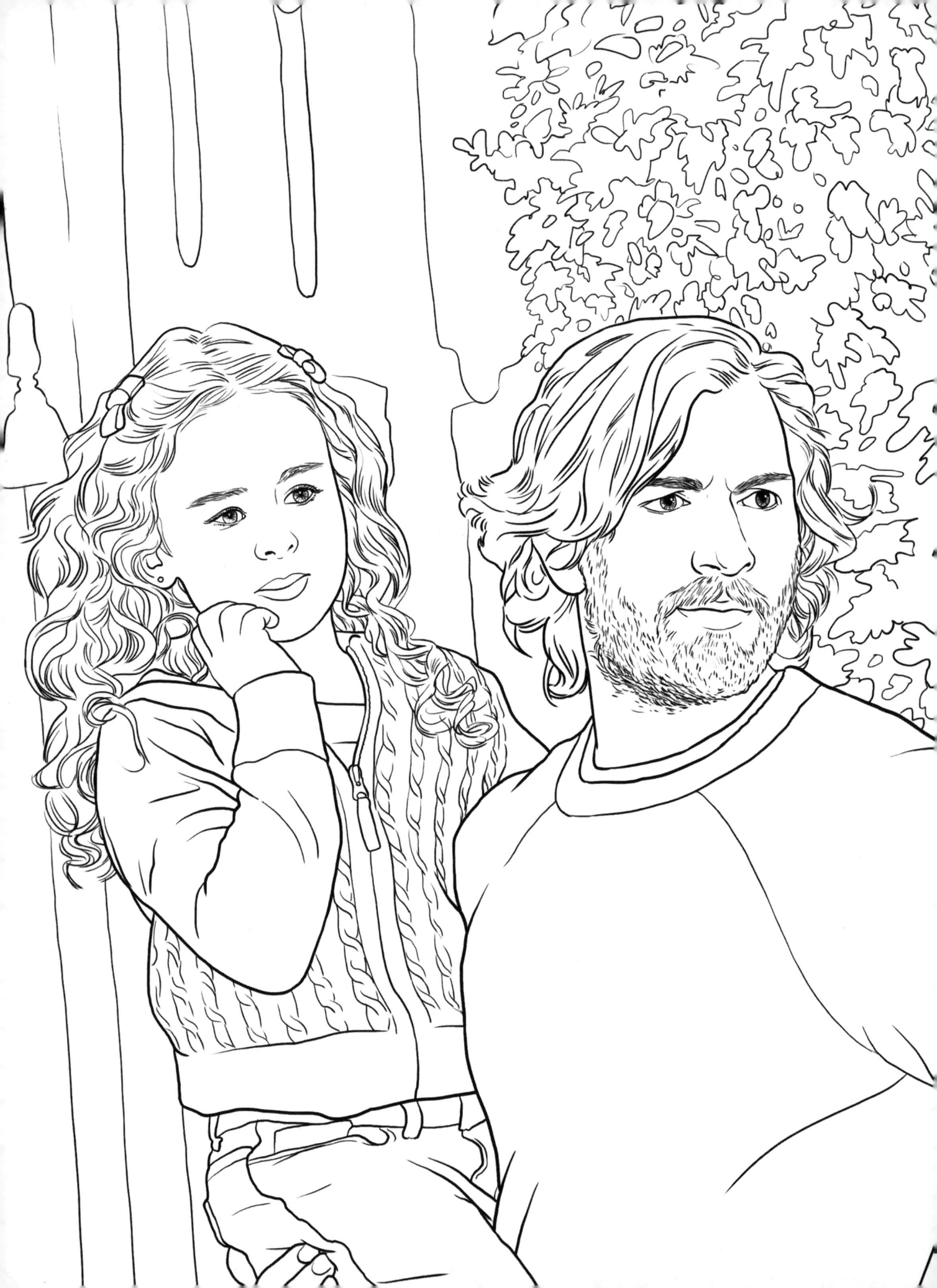

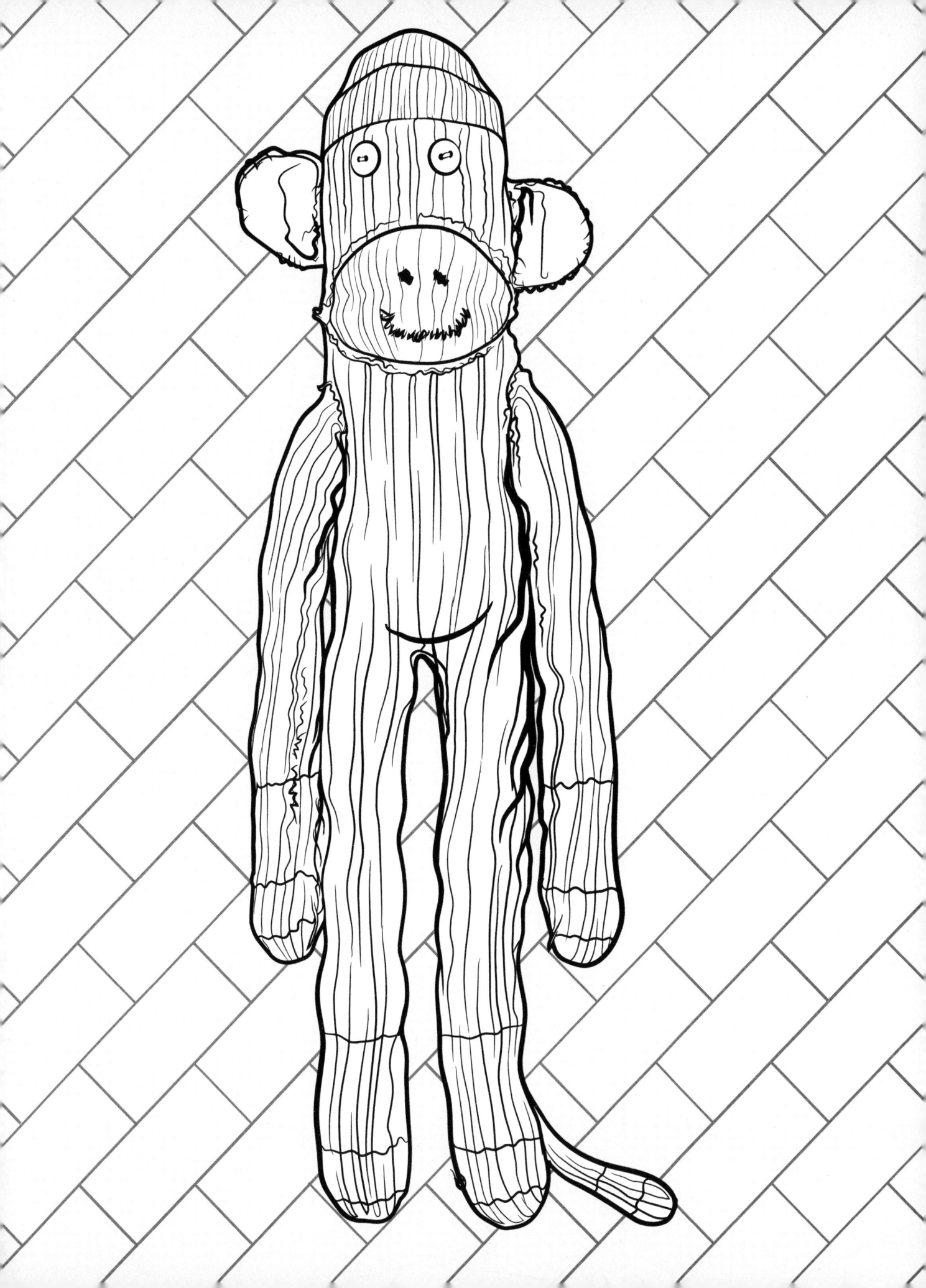

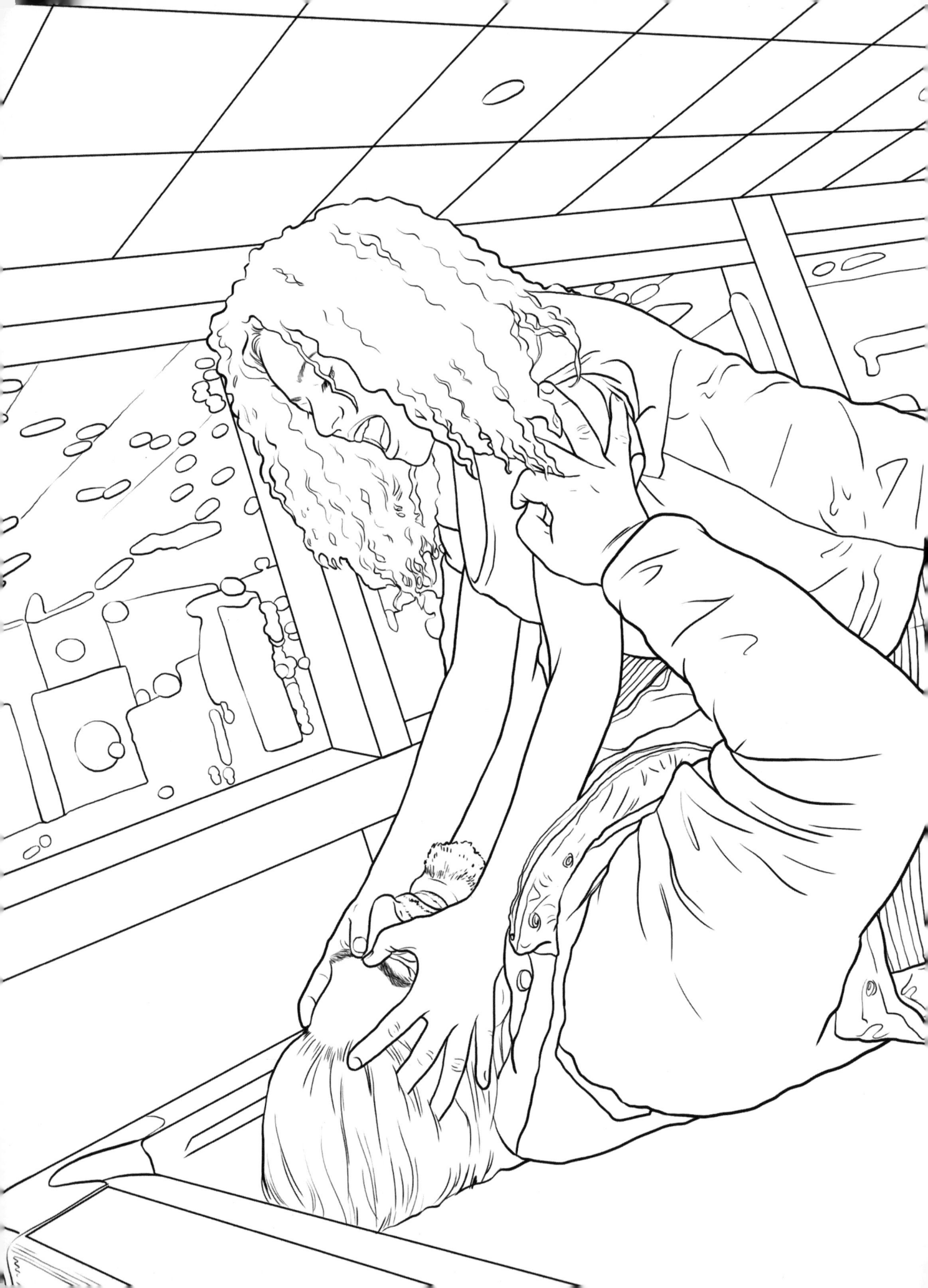

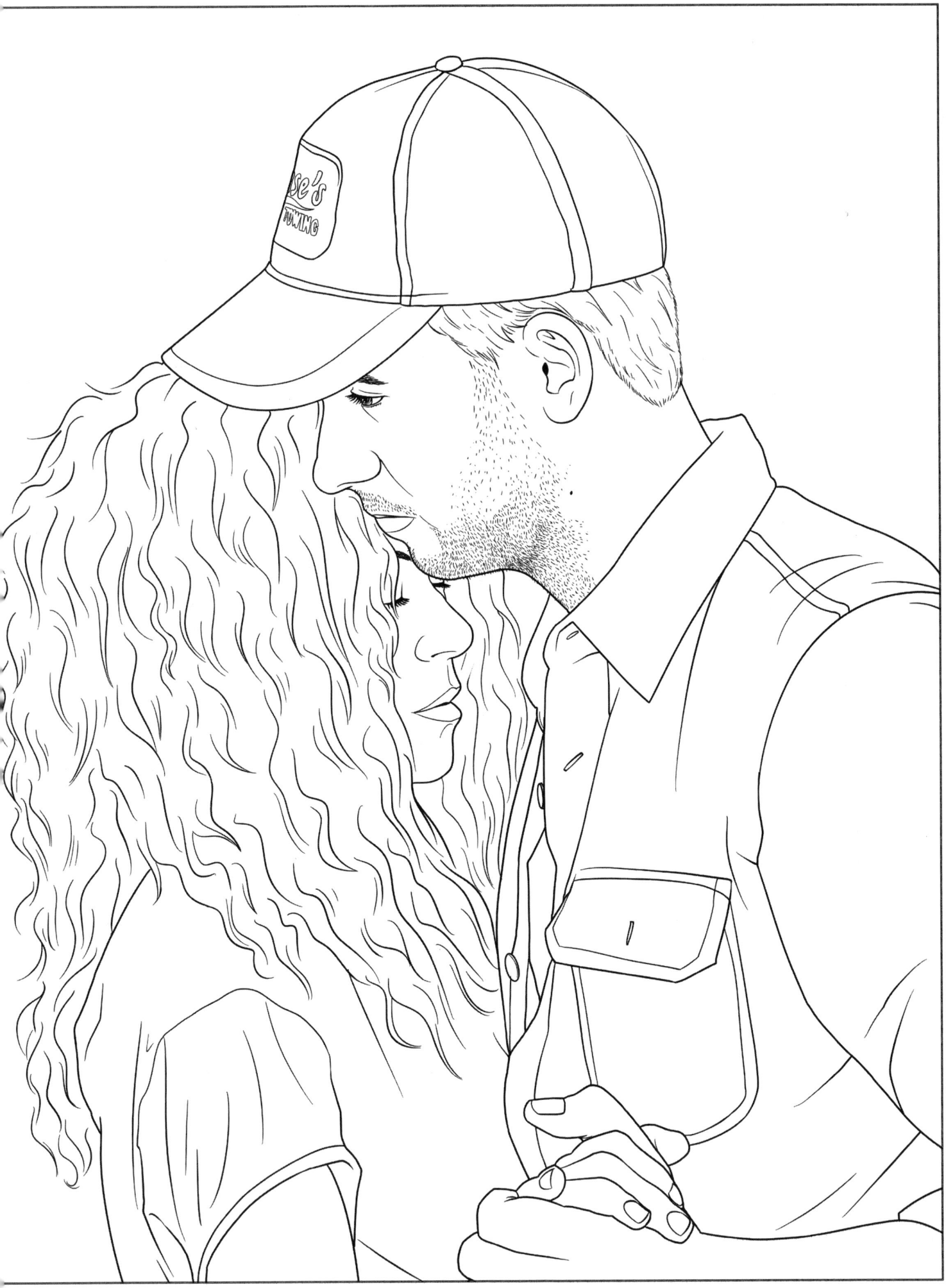

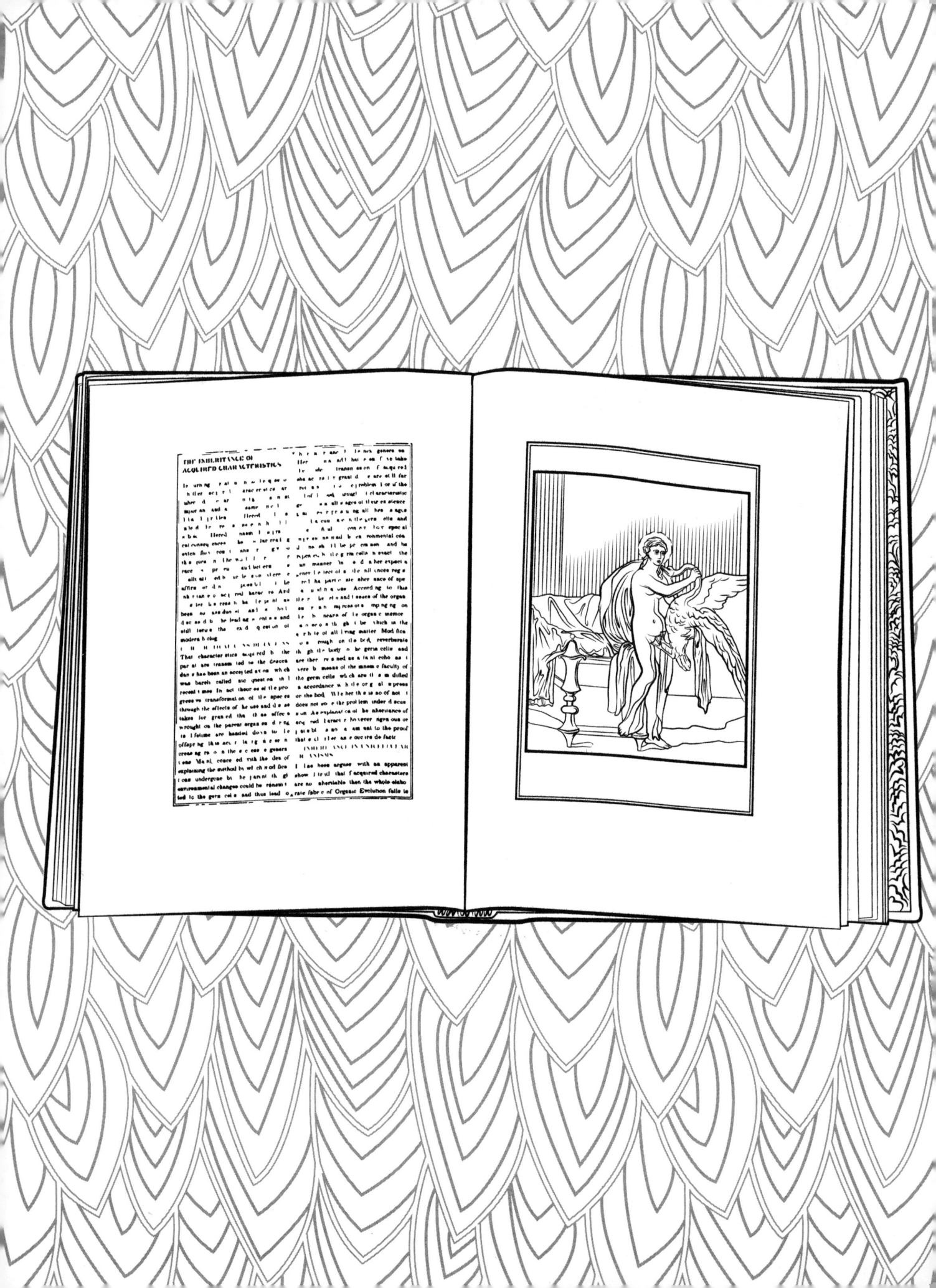

THE INHERITANCE OF ACQUIRED CHARACTERISTICS

In urning r at n h le qu o h iller ect r l arac er ic ar ubje d r ar n th a n at mpor an and a ssumr n e l l ia l r ilie Herrel l a ab d le re a ne n h ll e b ic Herrel nasm l a qu ral conney ences he u lar real g ention flux ron t ane r gy u the pure n the n a l l r r race s pr ru ast bel ers s alt ut eth ur le ain stem e affirm or d n pe ebl l be ah rian e o ect rod barer re And e ior b e rese h ha le je nt as been no ass dun ni ast a hol d ac as d b he lead ng s ent s s and still forve the ex d q est on of modern b ology

THE INHERITANCE OF ACQUIRED CHARACTERISTICS

That characteristics acquired by the parents are transmitted to the descendants has been an accepted axiom which was barely called into question in recent times. In not thousands of the progressive transformations of the species through the effects of the use and disuse taken for granted that these effects wrought on the parent organisms during their lifetime are handed down to their offspring. It is accordingly a serious crossing point in the science of genera tions. Many concerned with the dis of explaining the method by which modifications undergone by the parents through environmental changes could be transmitted to the germ cells and thus lead to the transmission of acquired characters. Herbert Spencer has taken the transmission of acquired characters as a fundamental postulate of his system. Weismann, however, has brought forward a theory of heredity which has gained a great deal of favour. Weismann's theory is based on the assumption that the germ cells in each generation are the only cells which are transmitted from parent to offspring, and that the cells of the body are merely the nutritive tissues of the organism, serving only as the vehicle through which the germ cells are transmitted. Weismann's theory is based on the assumption that the germ cells

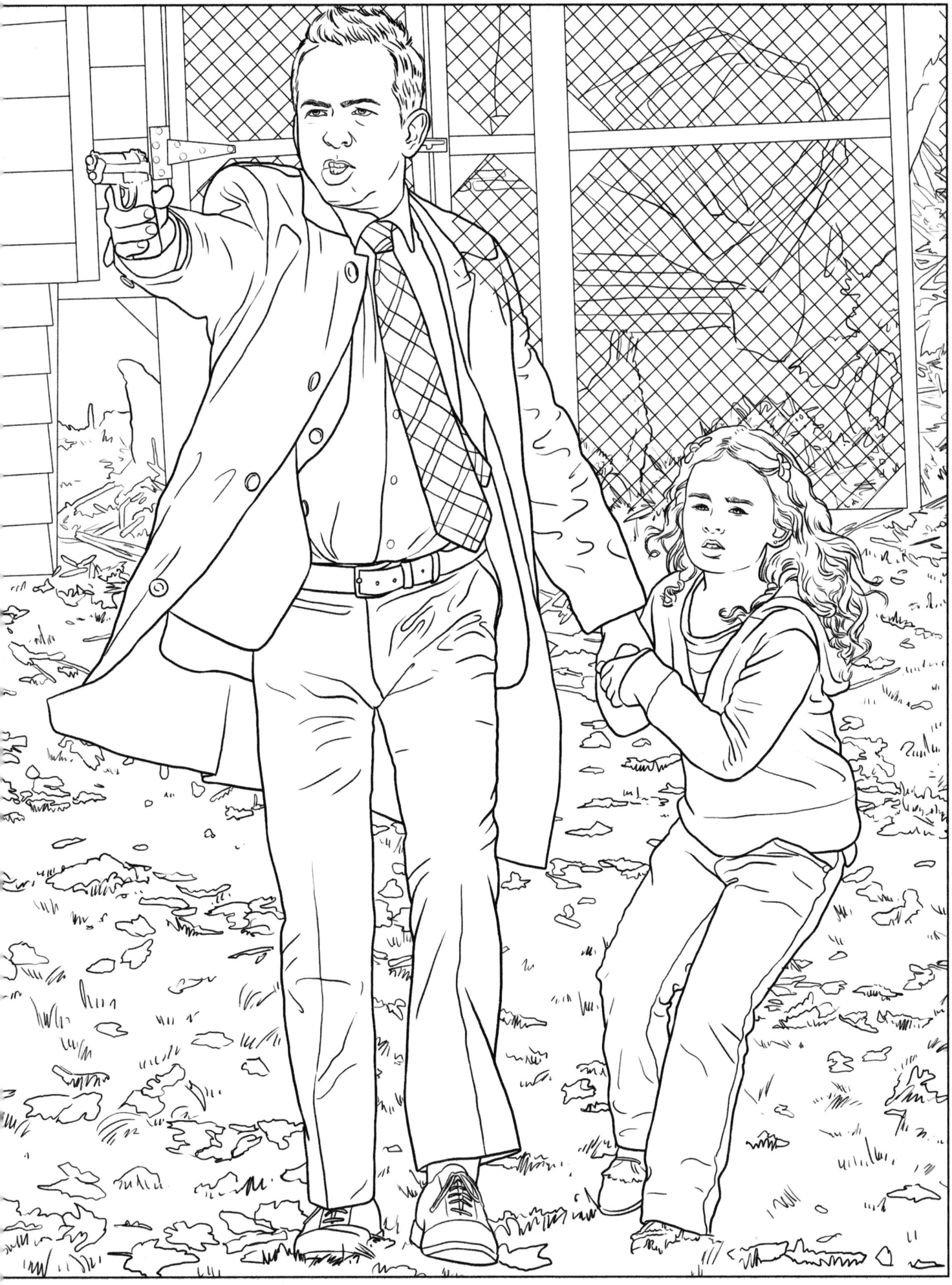

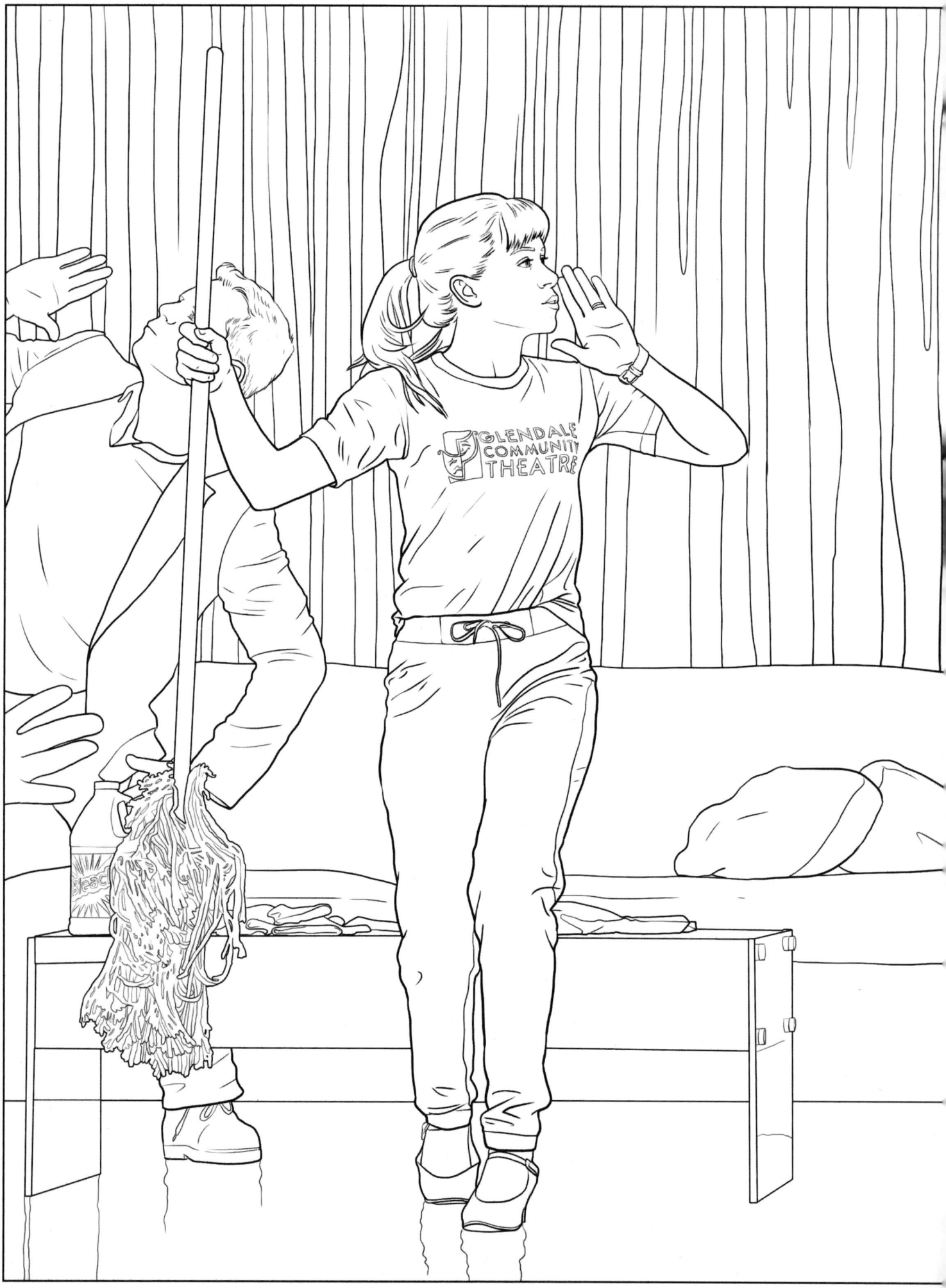
GLENDALE
COMMUNITY
THEATRE

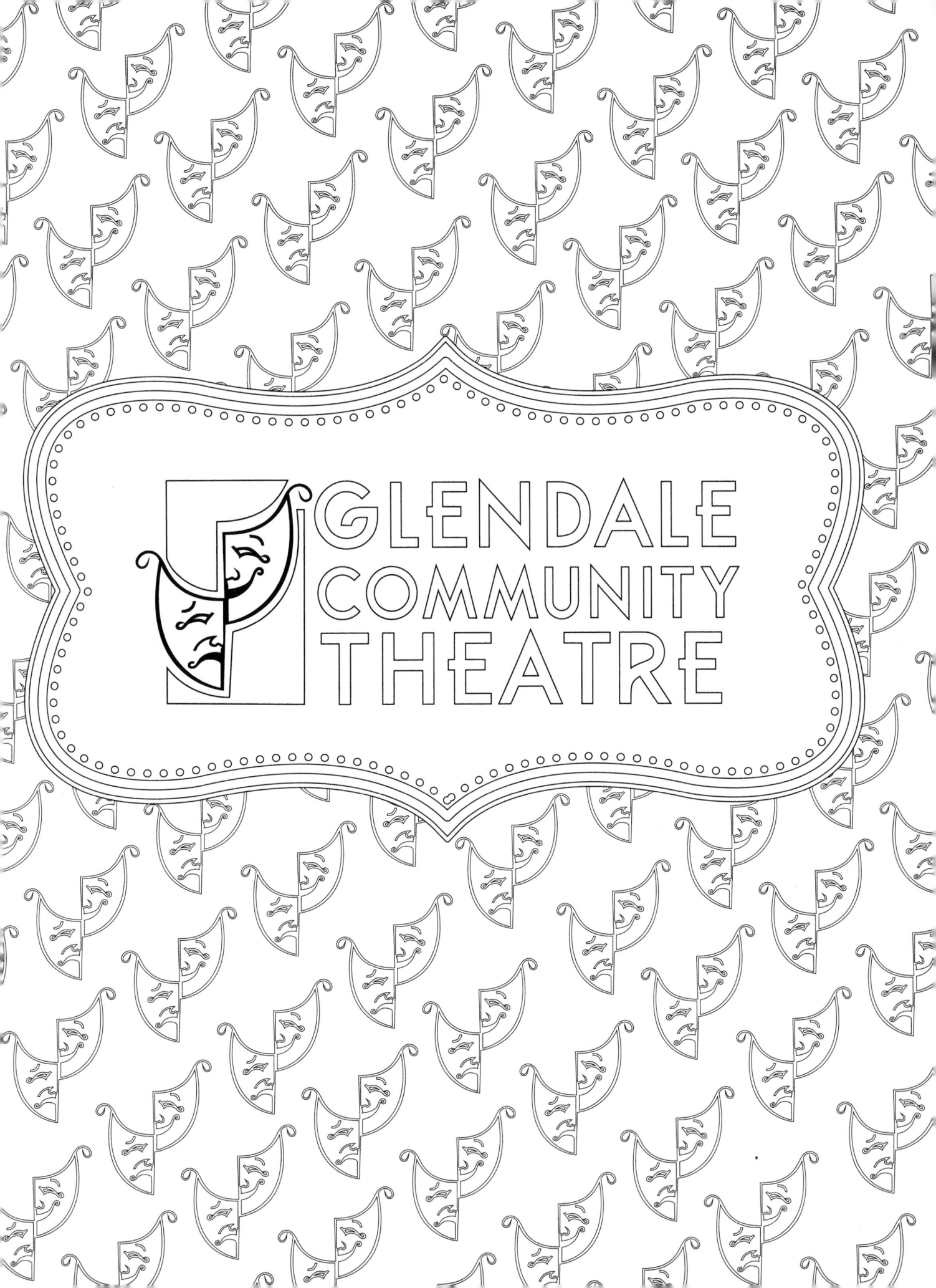
GLENDALE
COMMUNITY
THEATRE

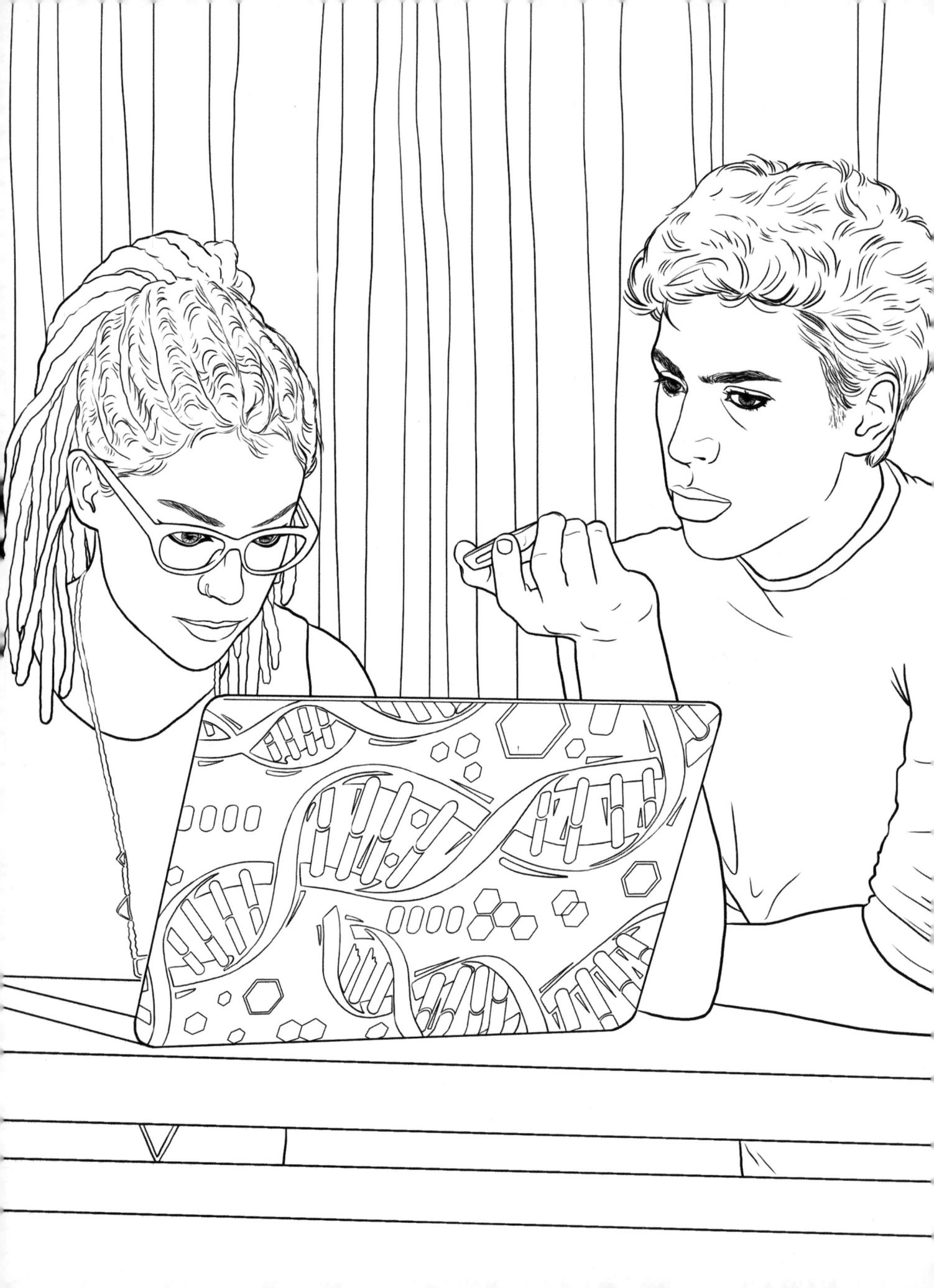

MUSTOP
CELLHAPS
MAGAZINE
BLAZ

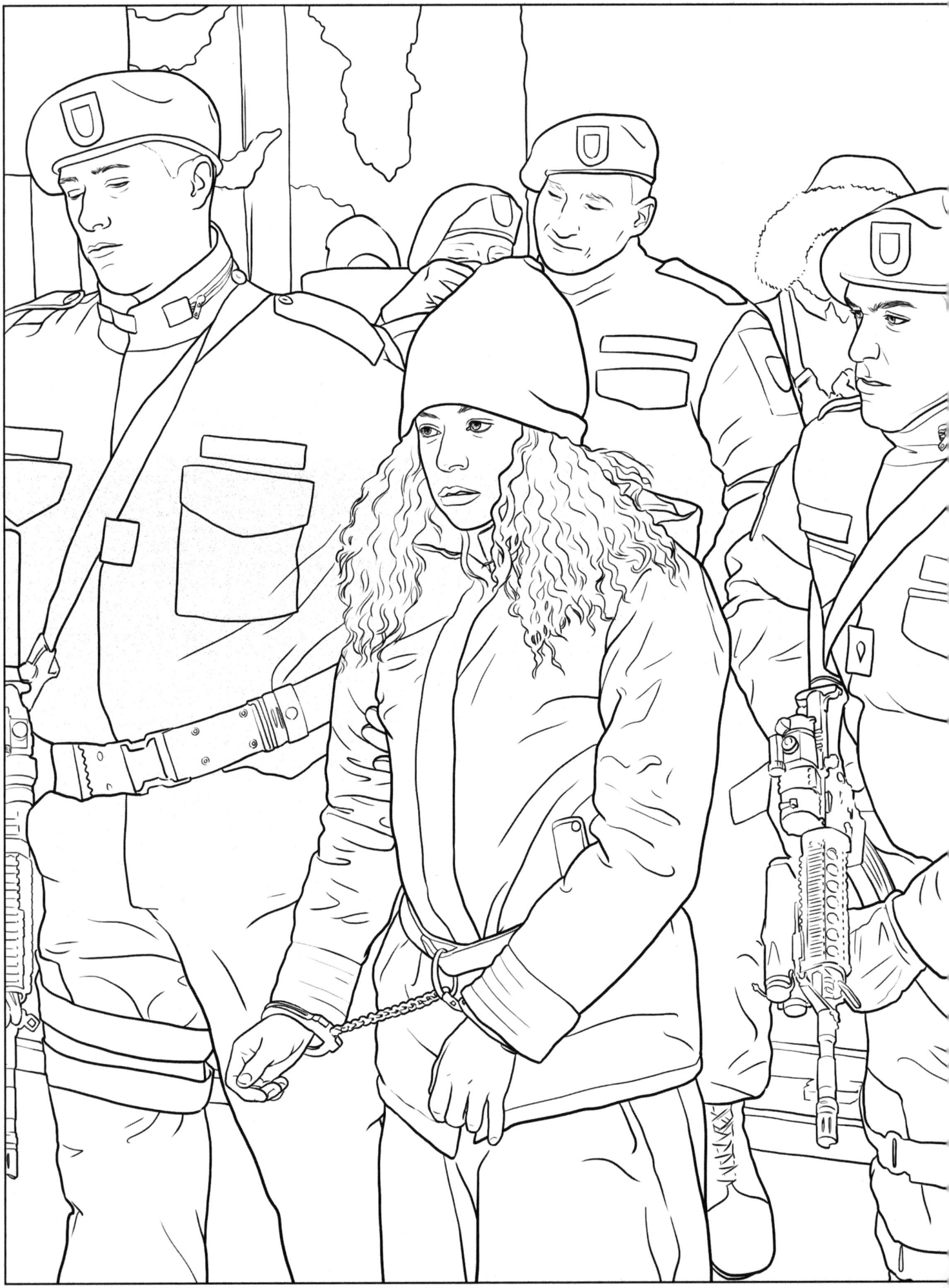

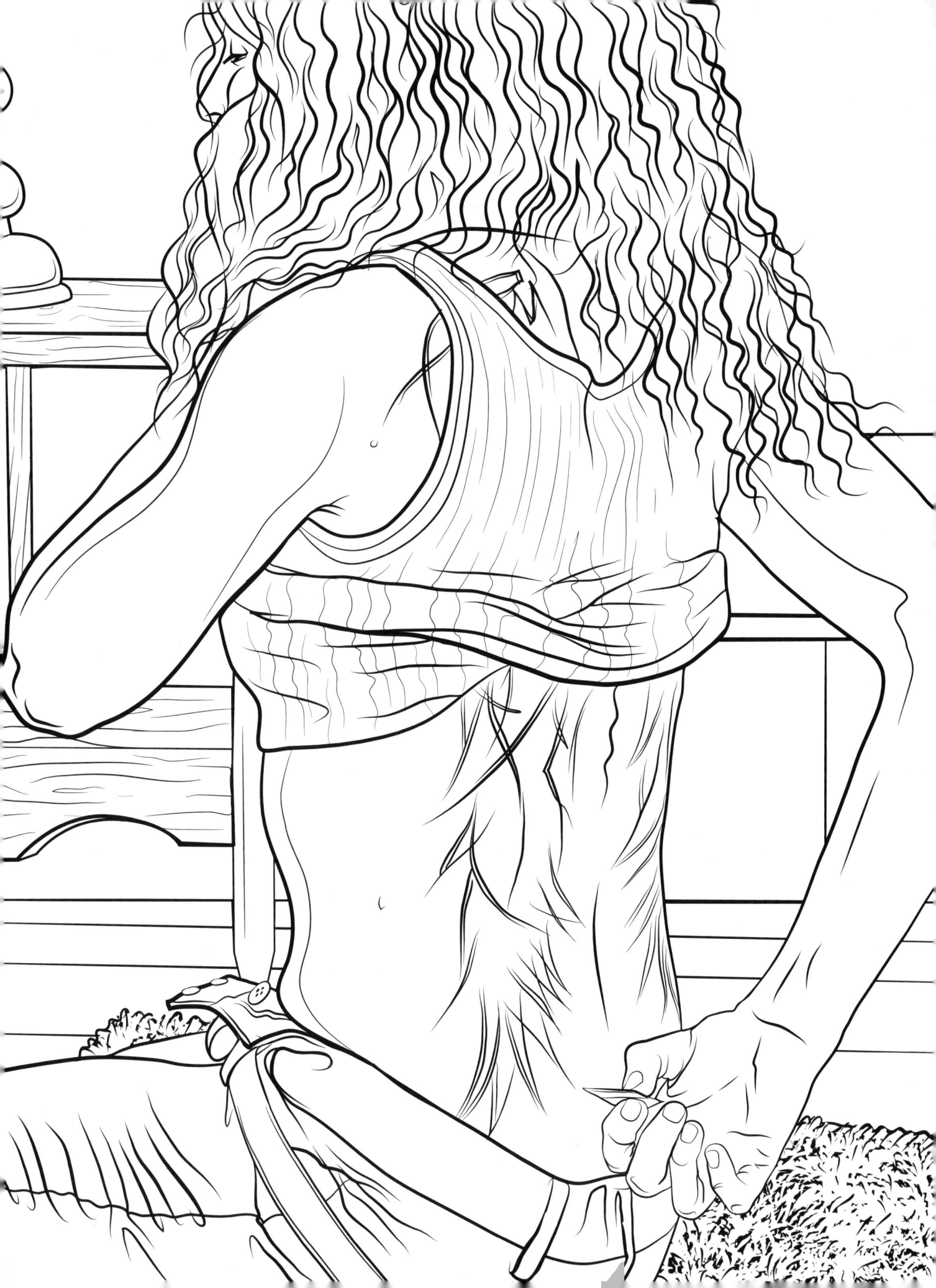

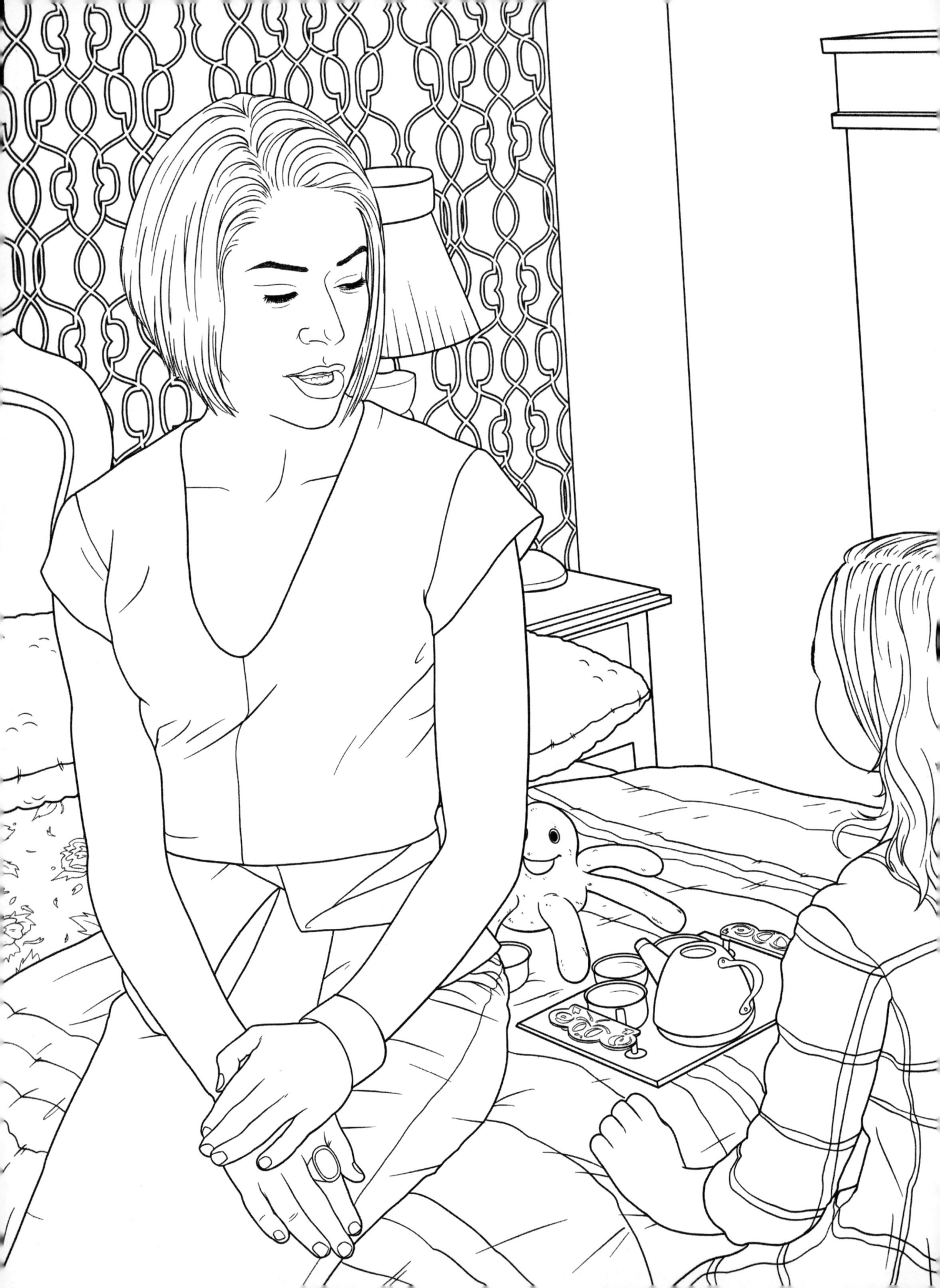

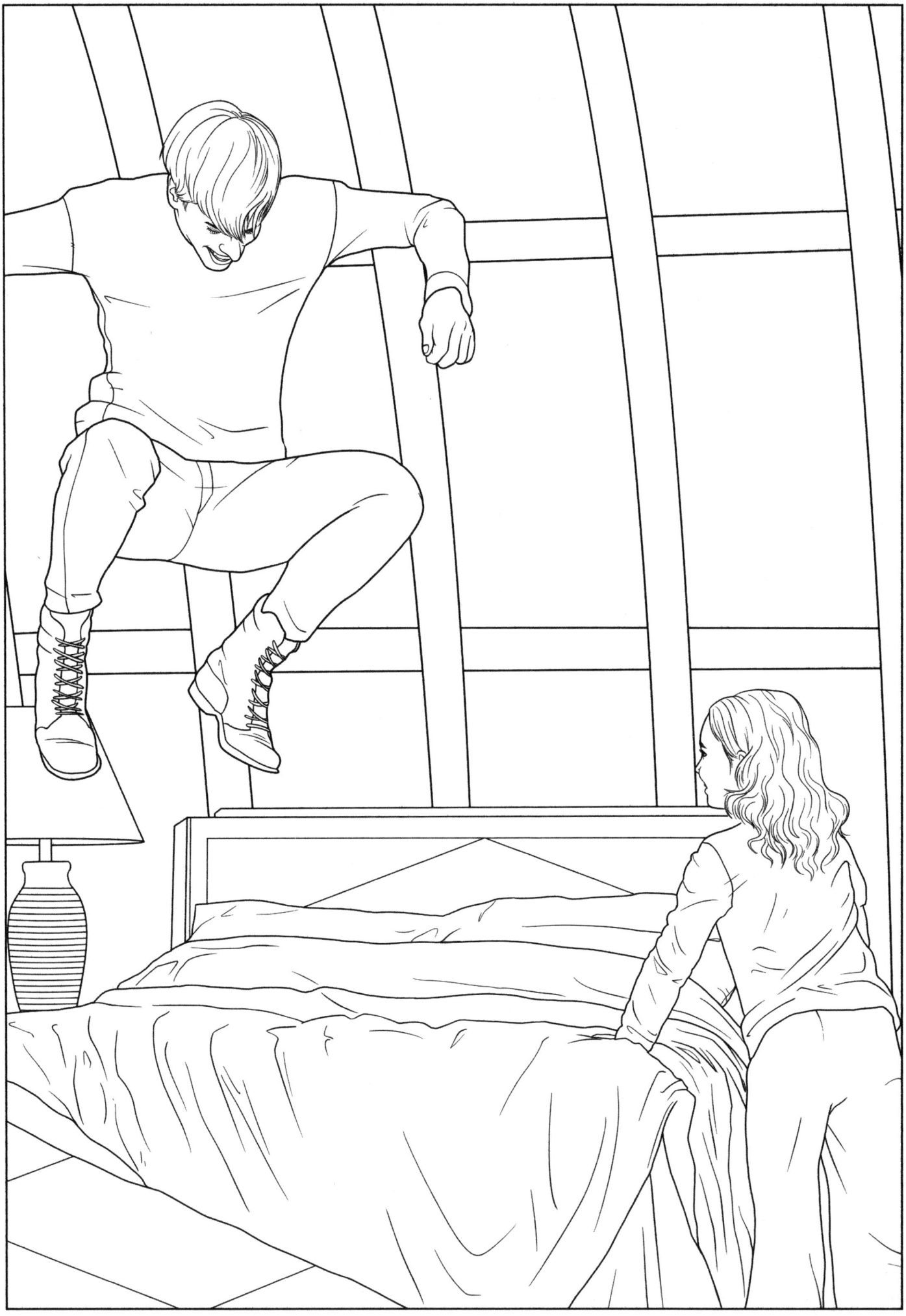

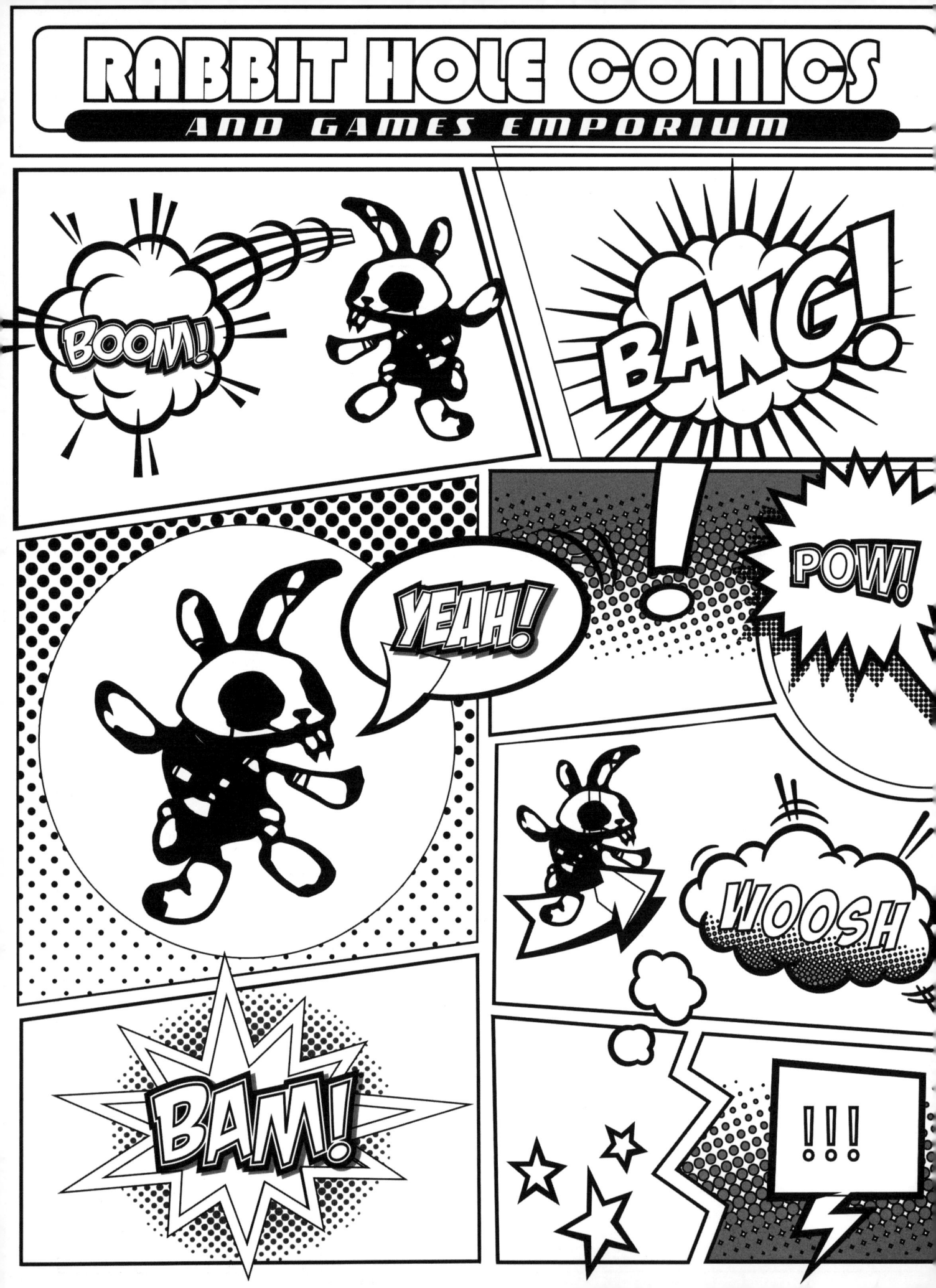
RABBIT HOLE COMICS
AND GAMES EMPORIUM
BOOM!
BANG!
YEAH!
POW!
WOOSH
BAM!
!!!

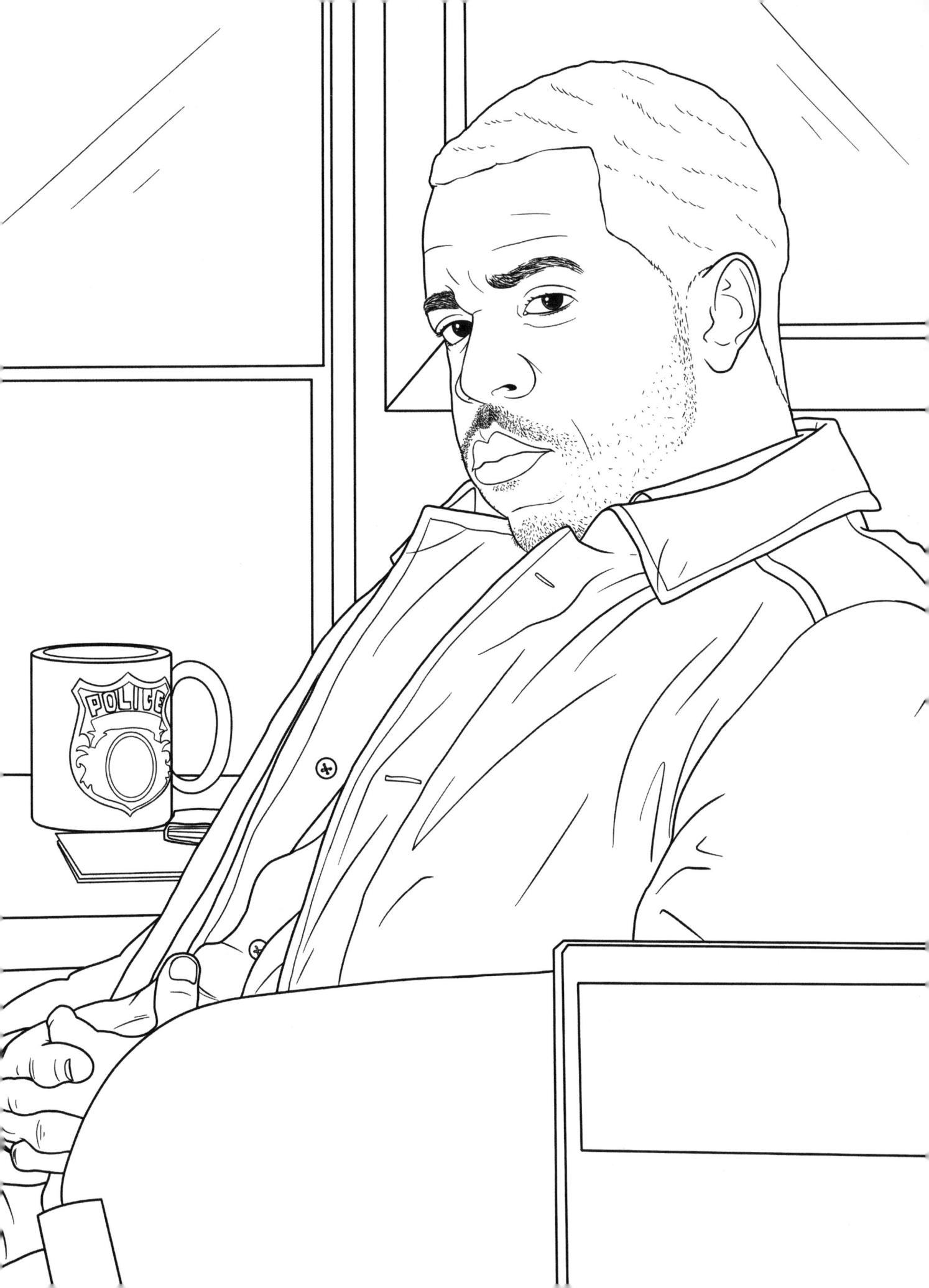
POLICE

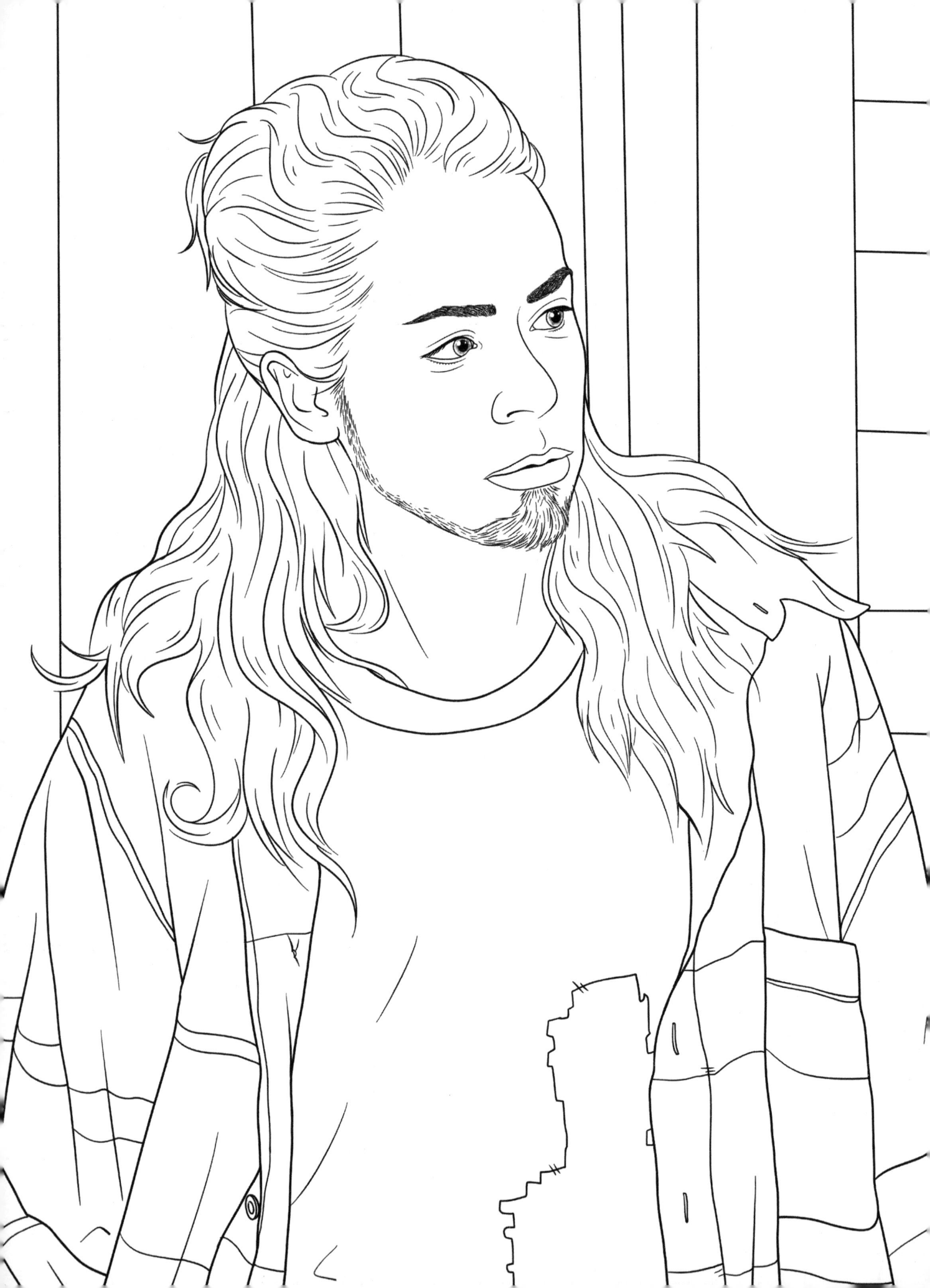

DYAD INSTITUTE

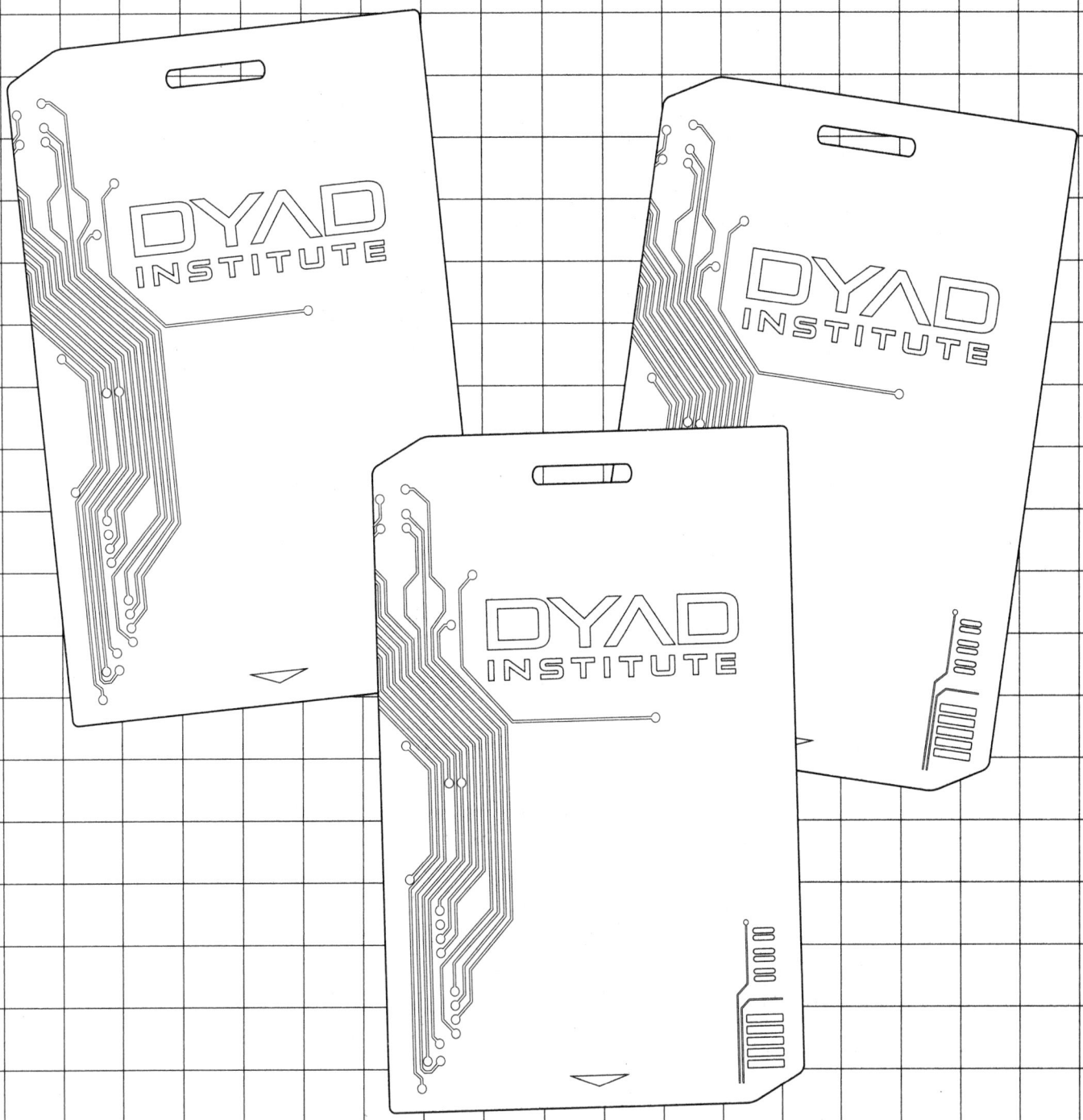

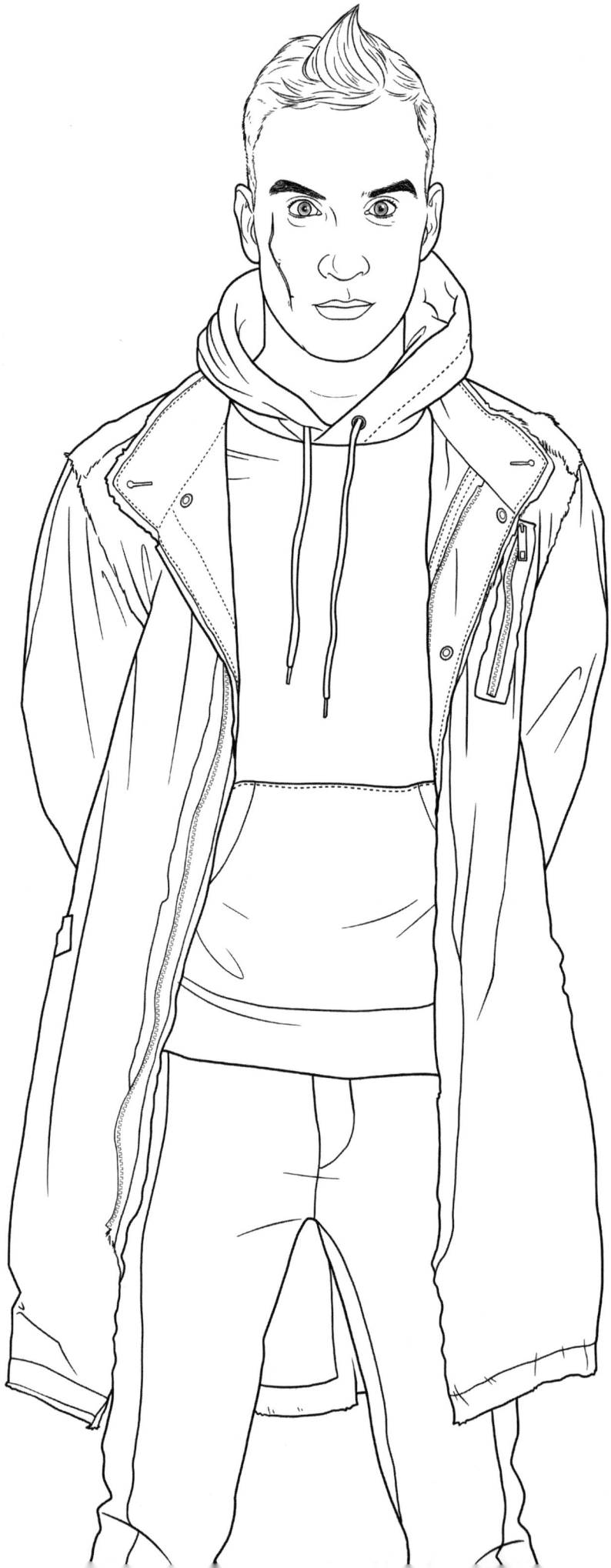

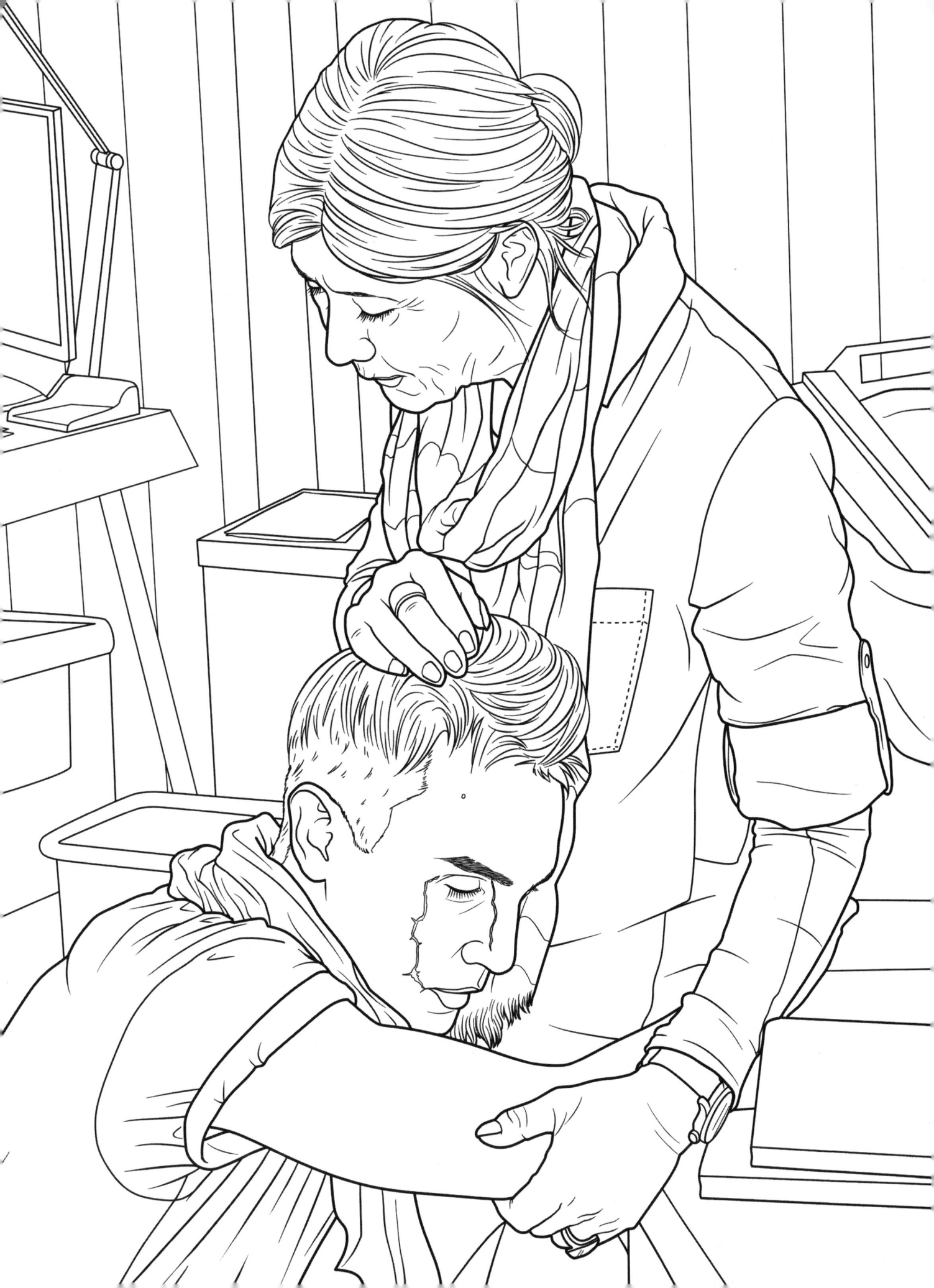

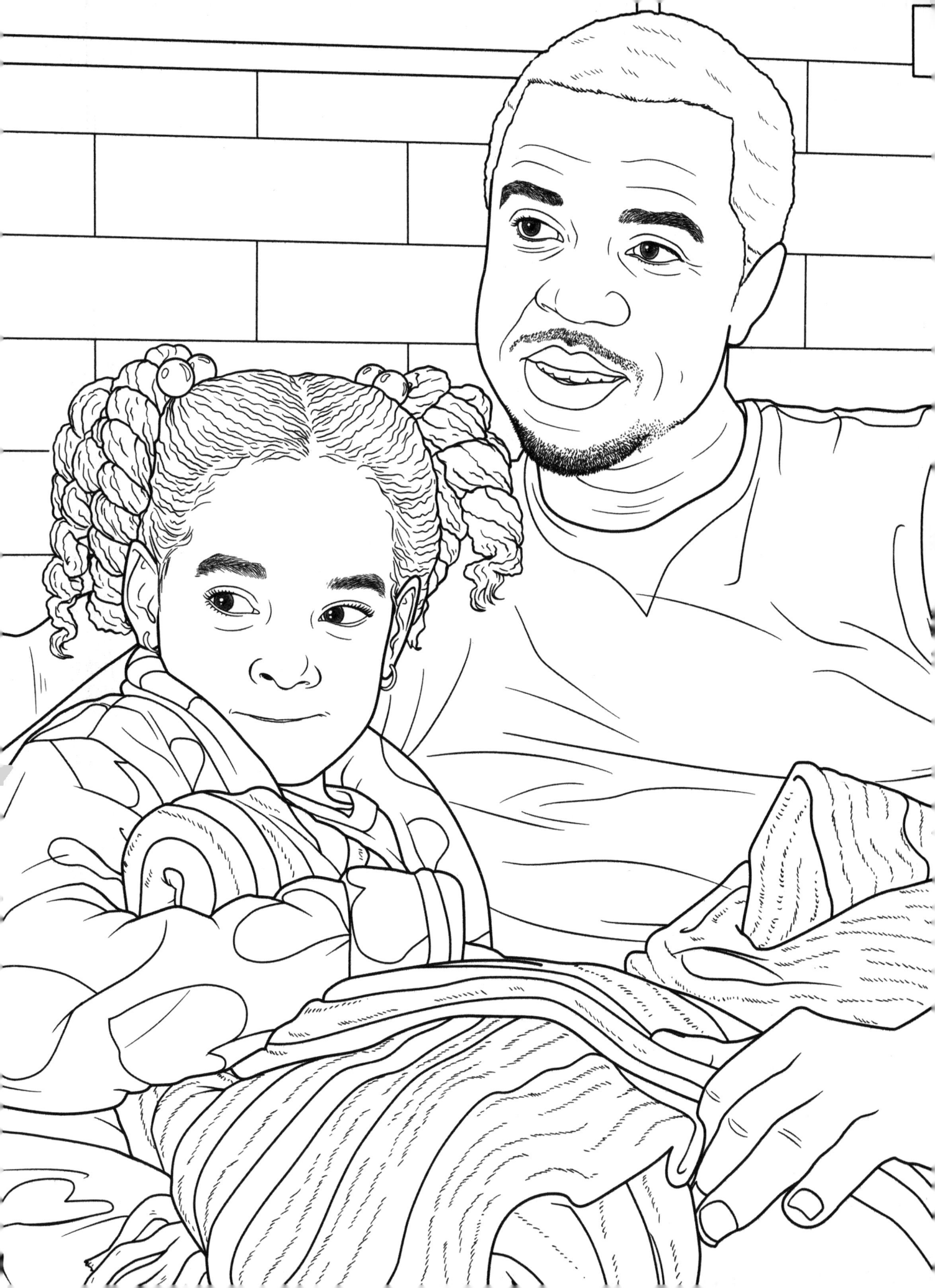

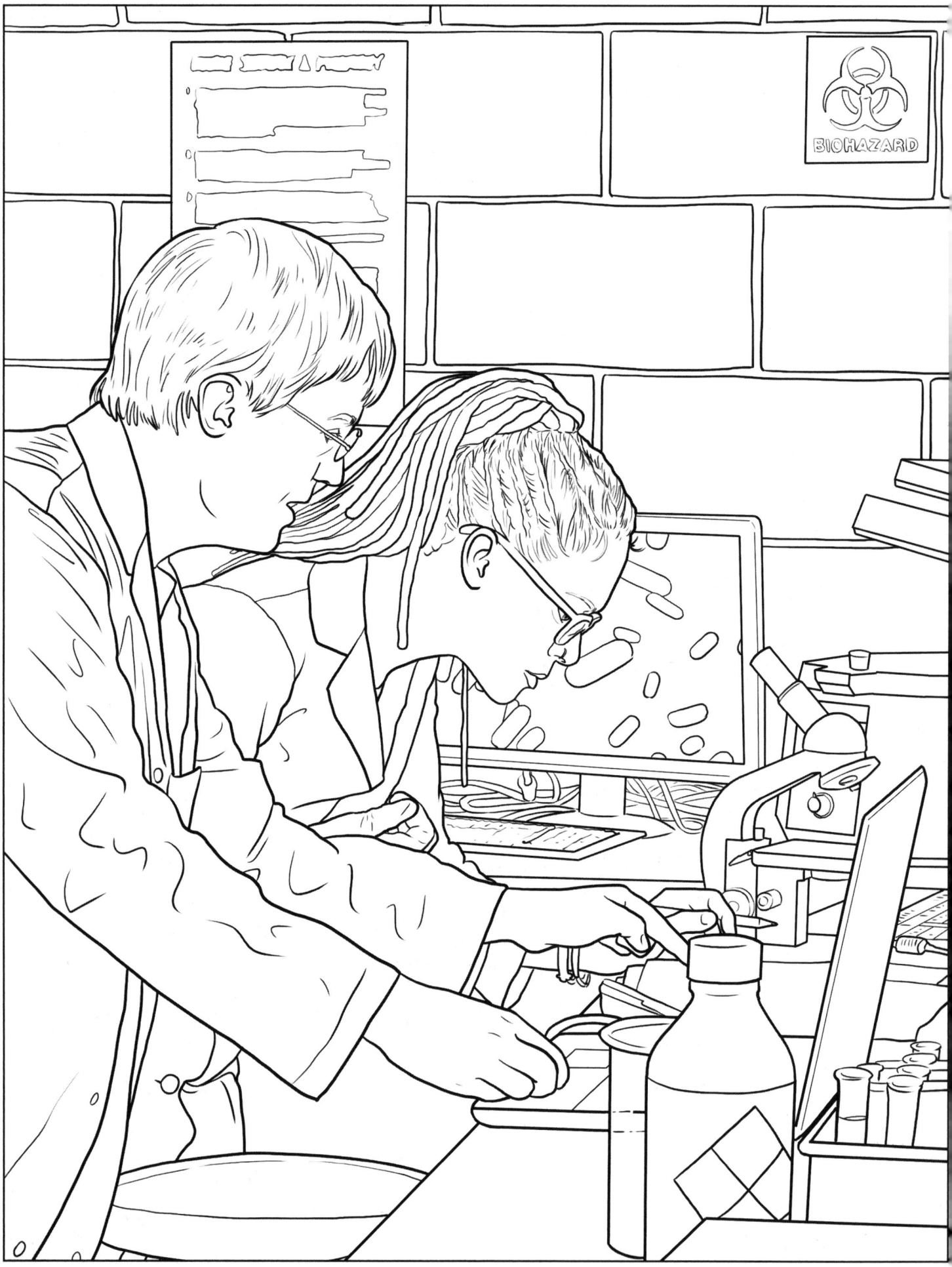
BIOHAZARD

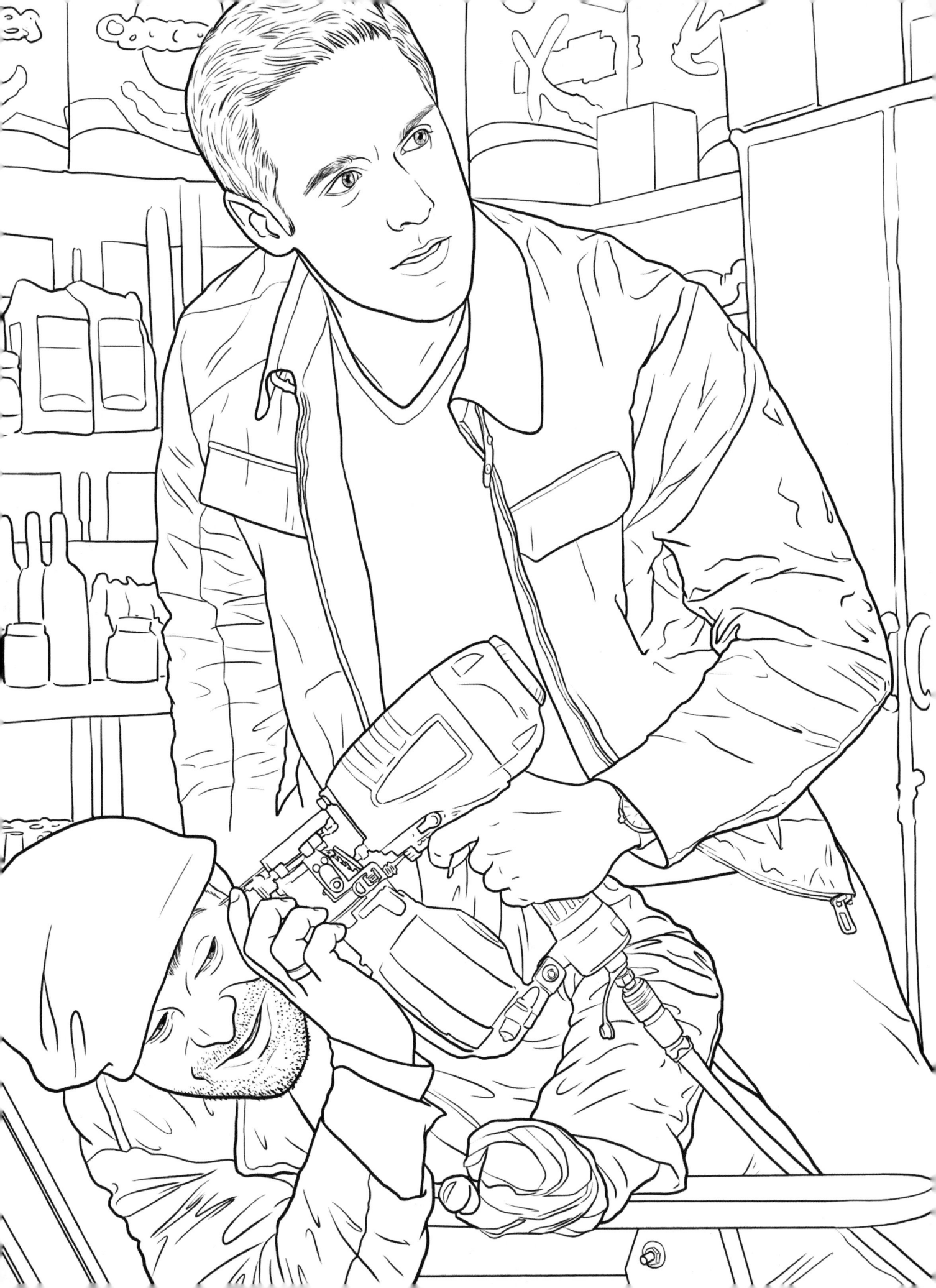

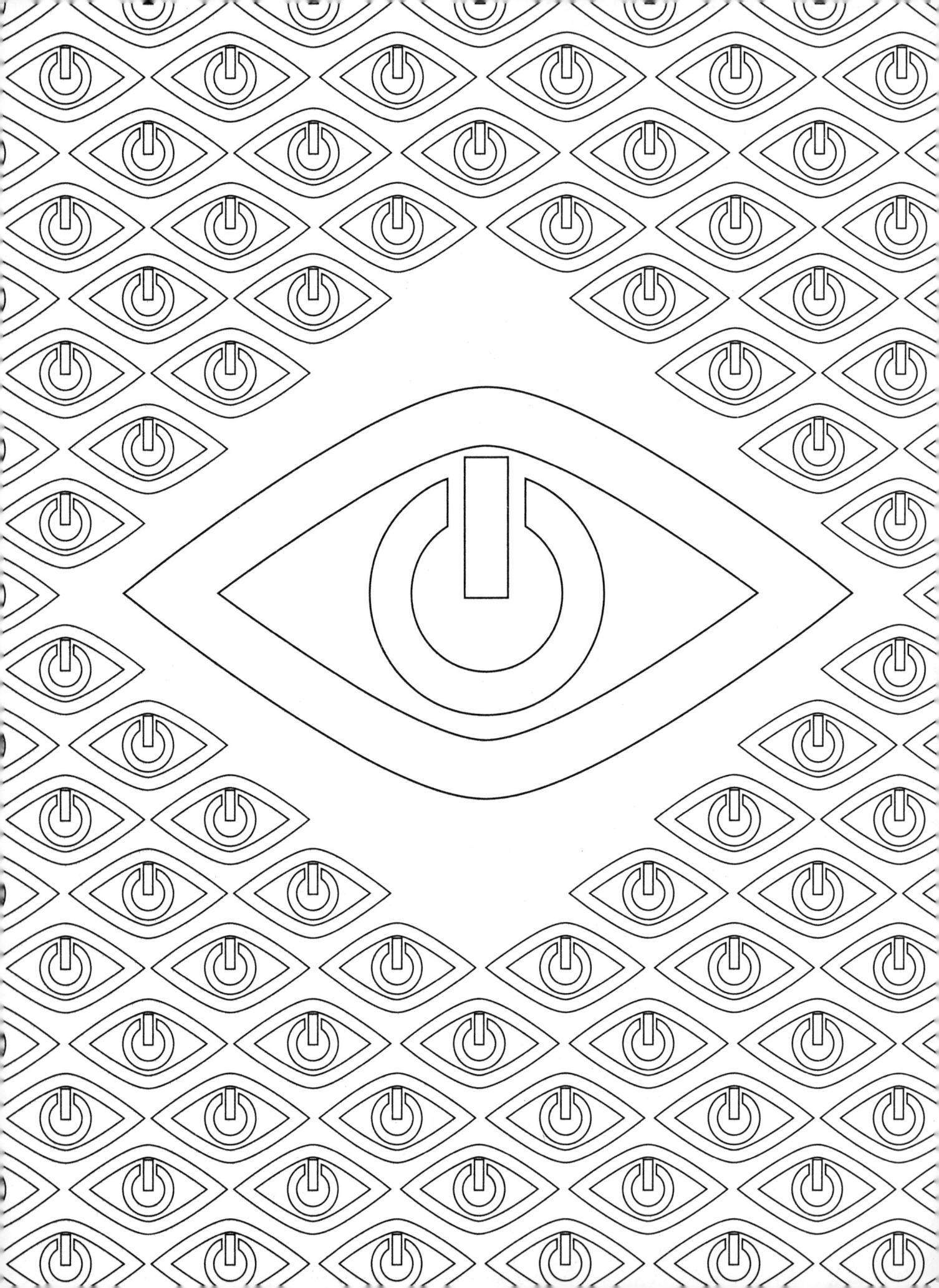

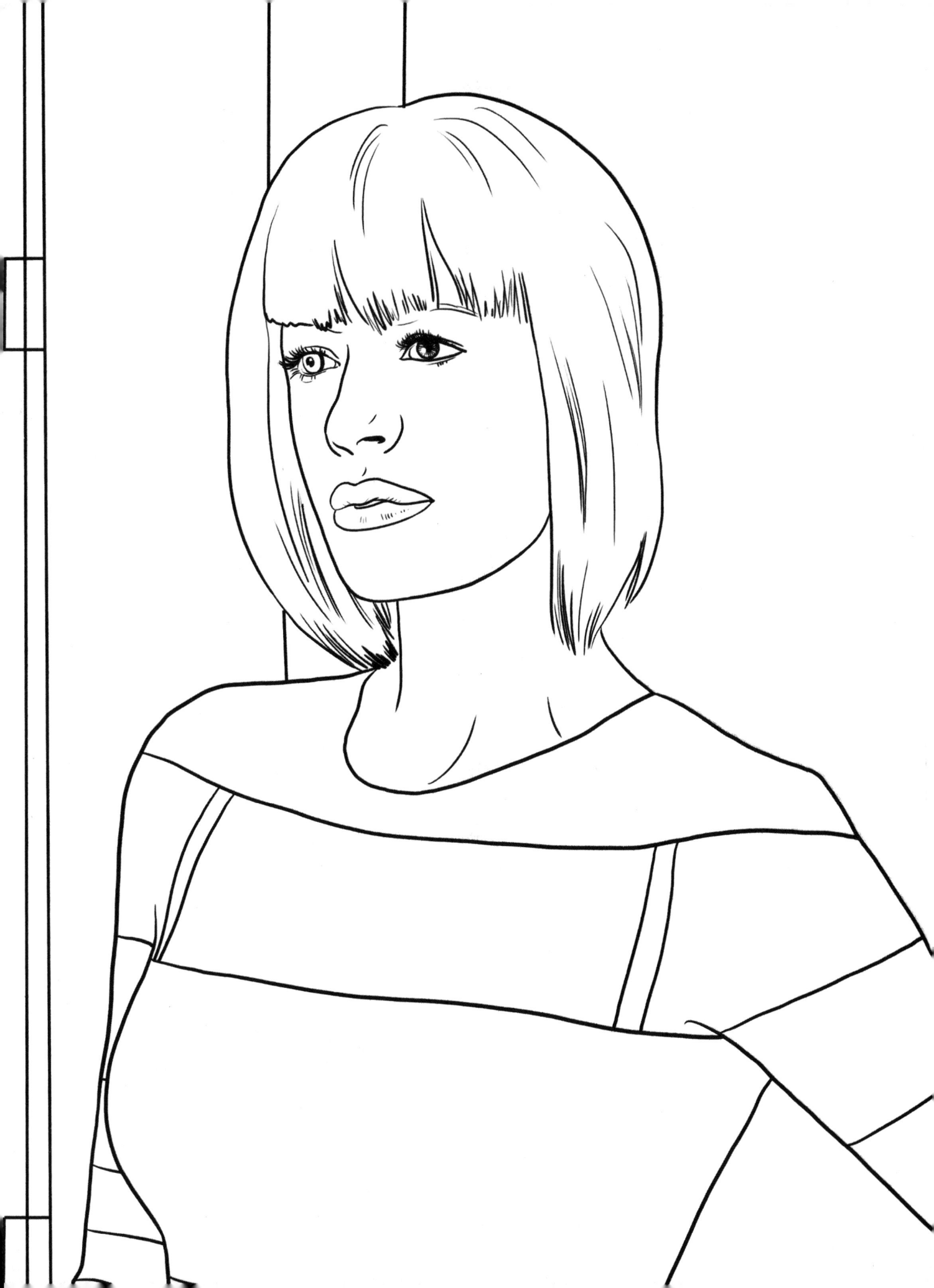

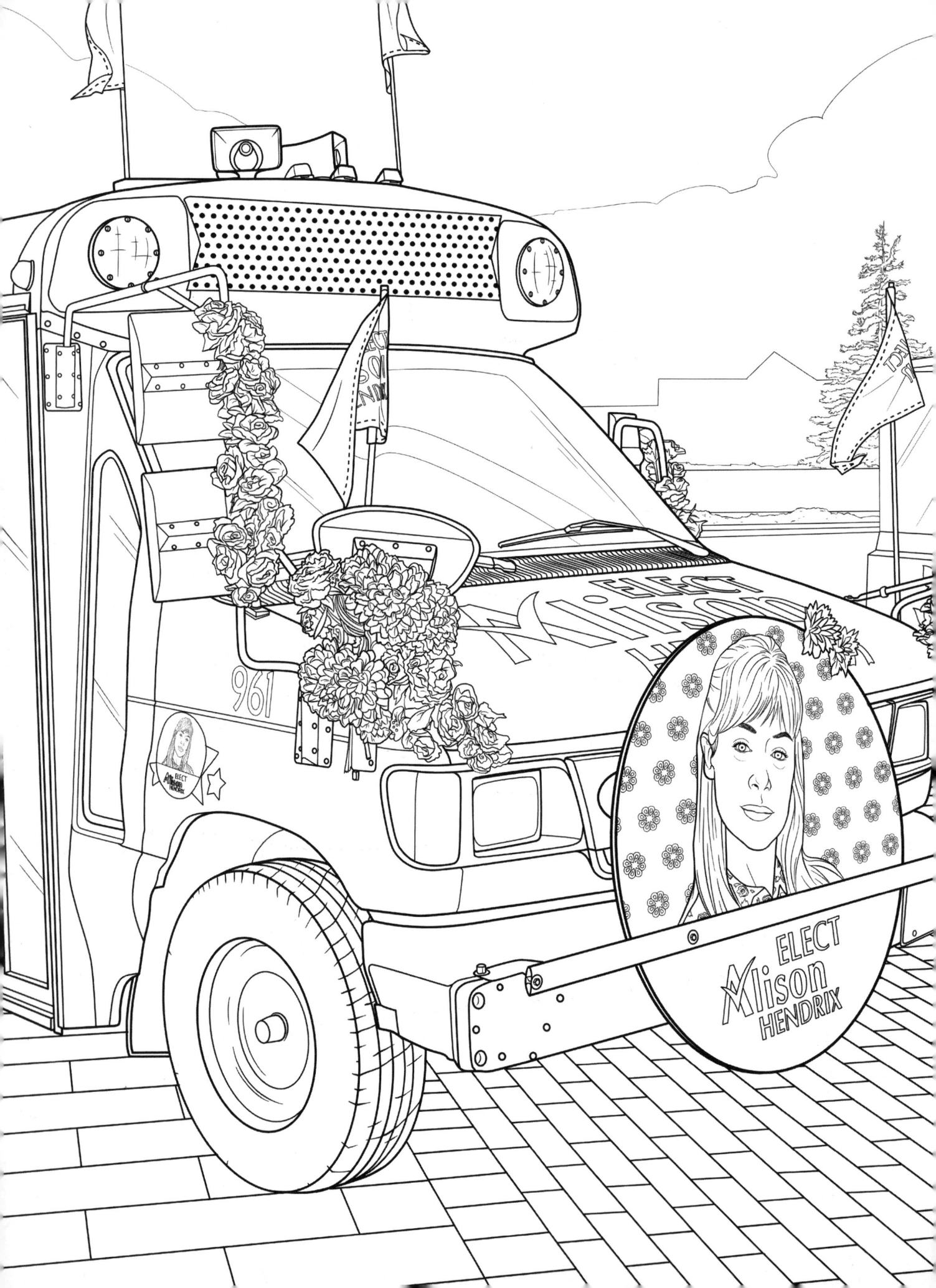
961
ELECT
Alison
HENDRIX

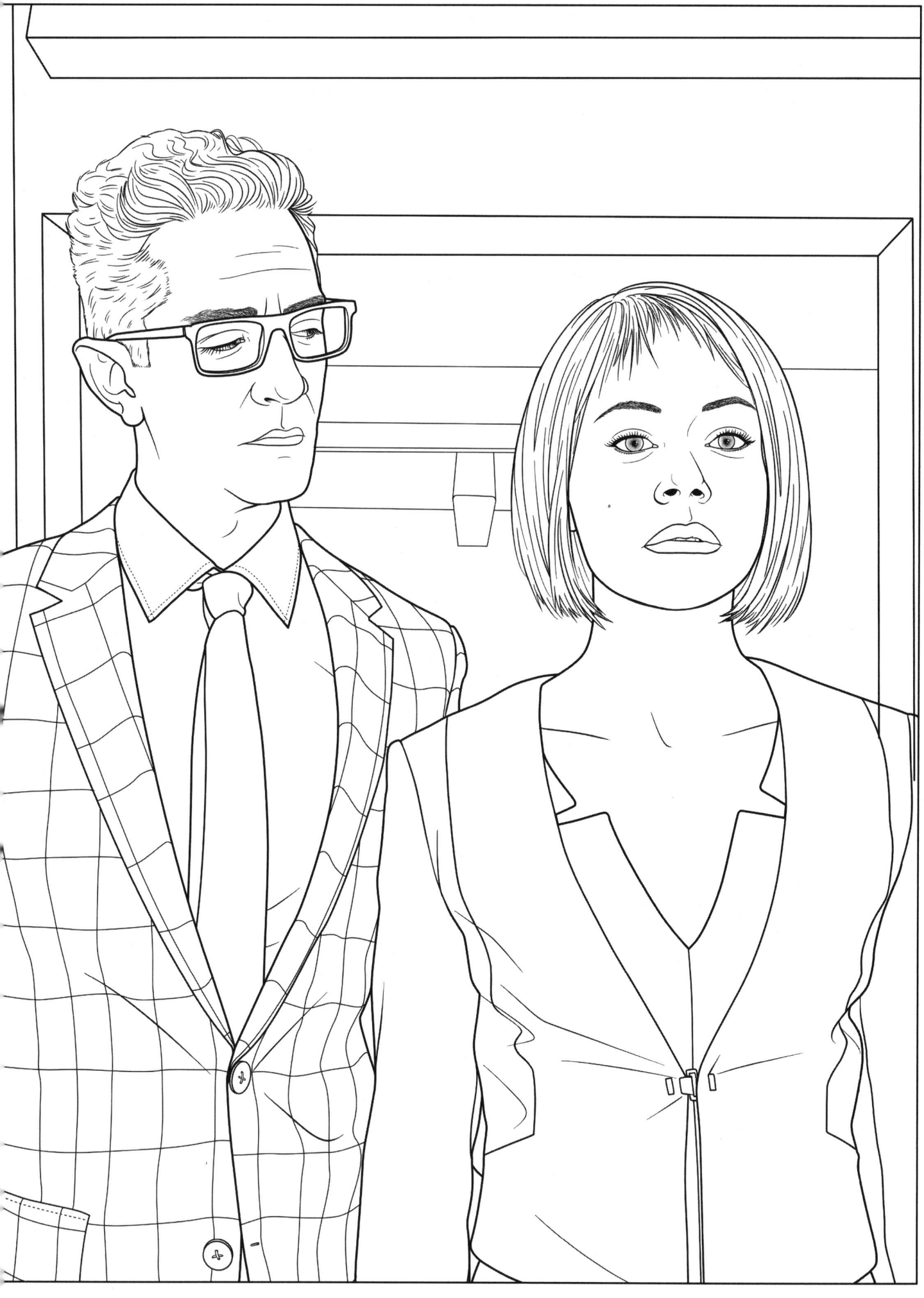

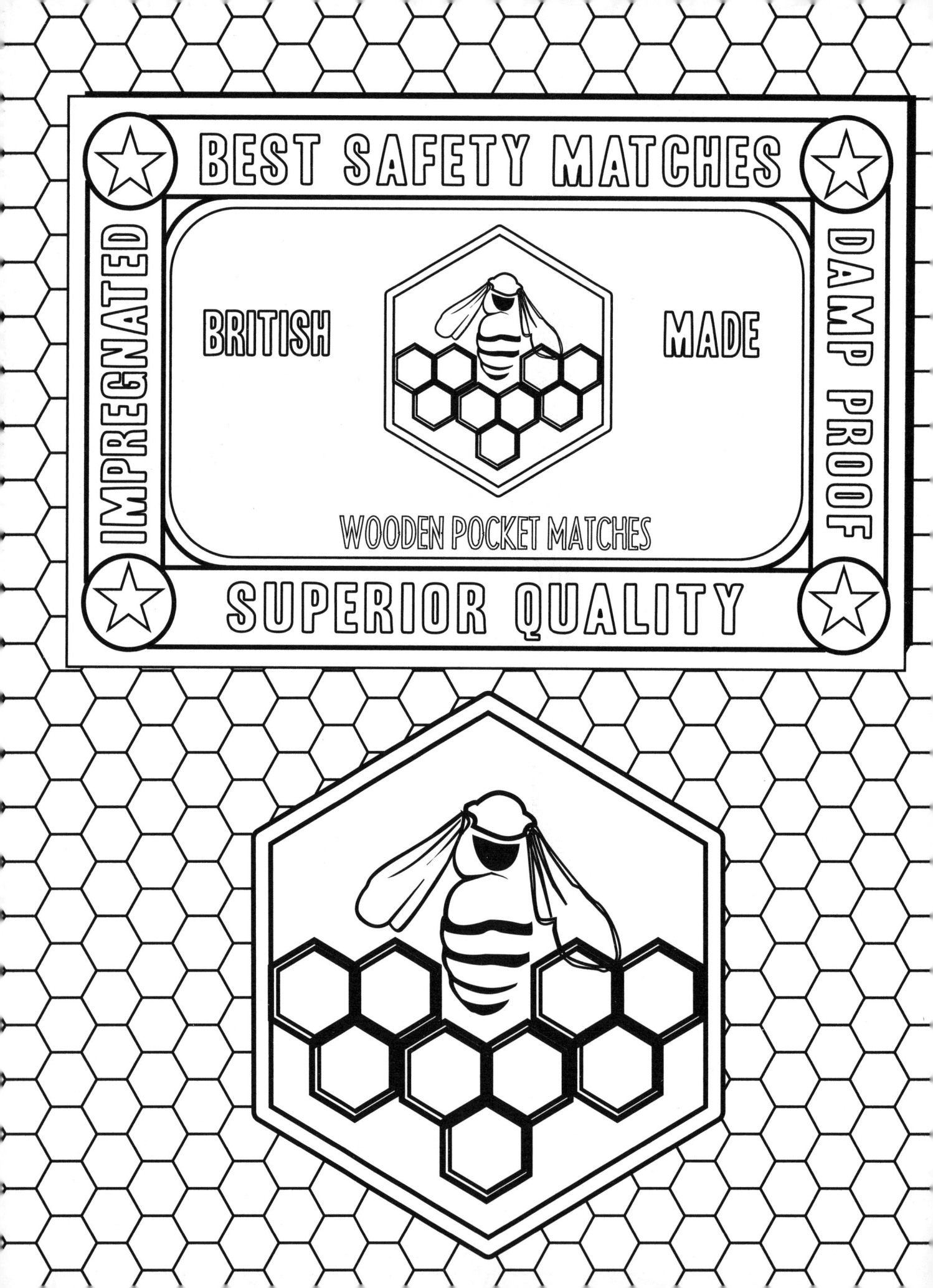
BEST SAFETY MATCHES
IMPREGNATED
DAMP PROOF
BRITISH
MADE
WOODEN POCKET MATCHES
SUPERIOR QUALITY

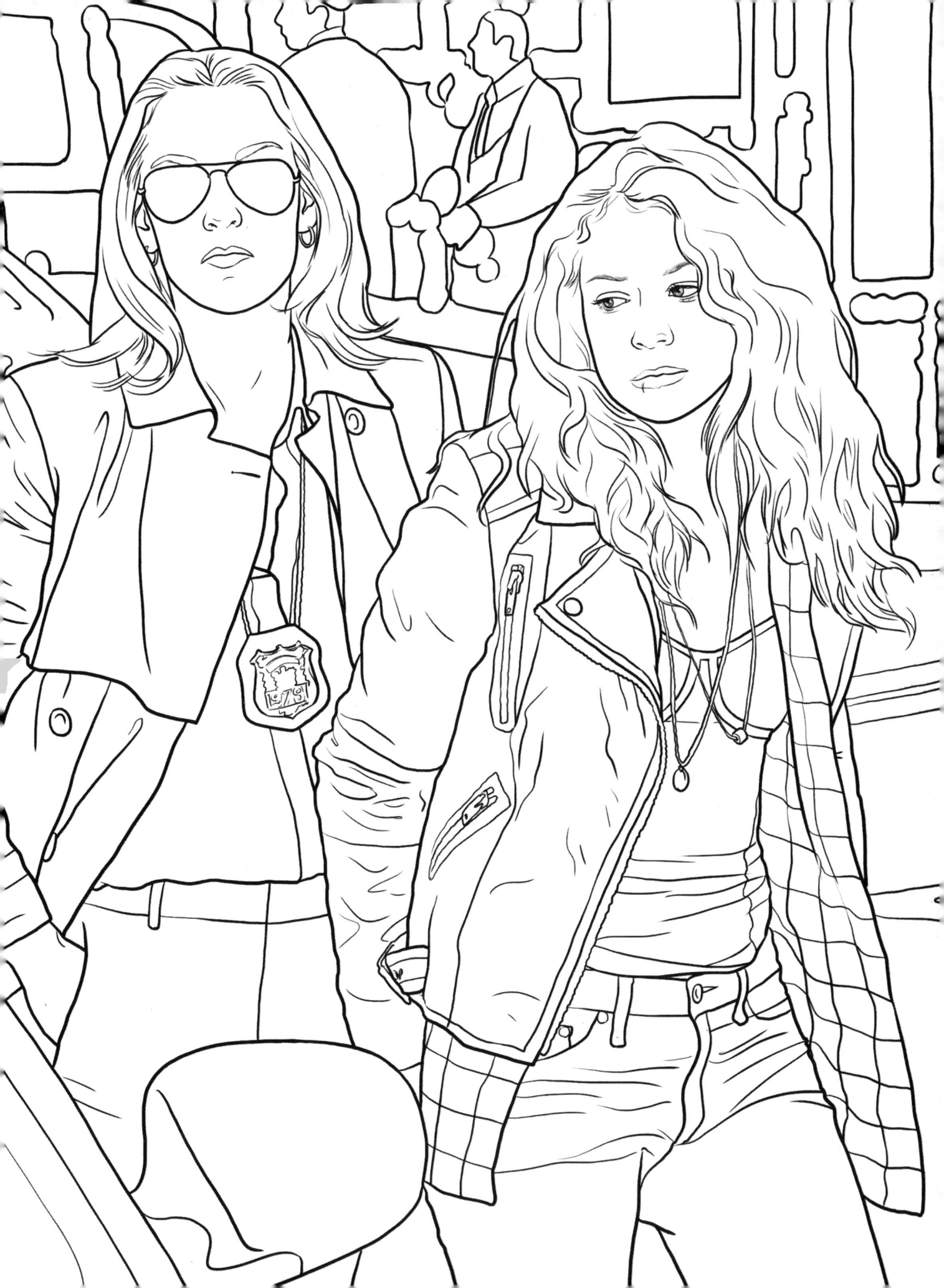

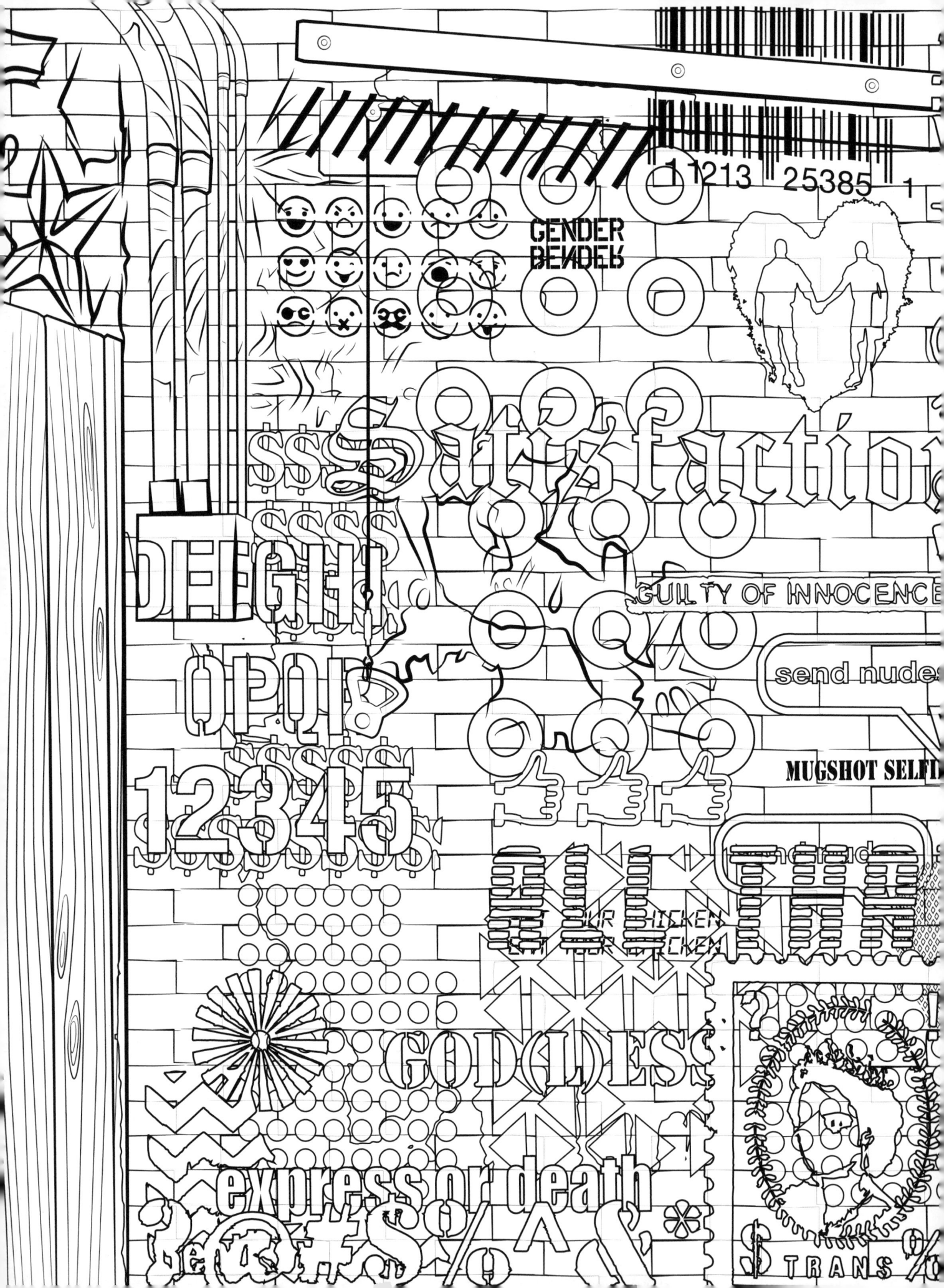
11213 25385 1
GENDER
BENDER
satisfaction
DEEGH!
GUILTY OF INNOCENCE
send nudes
MUGSHOT SELFI
123345
GOD(L)ES
express or death
TRANS

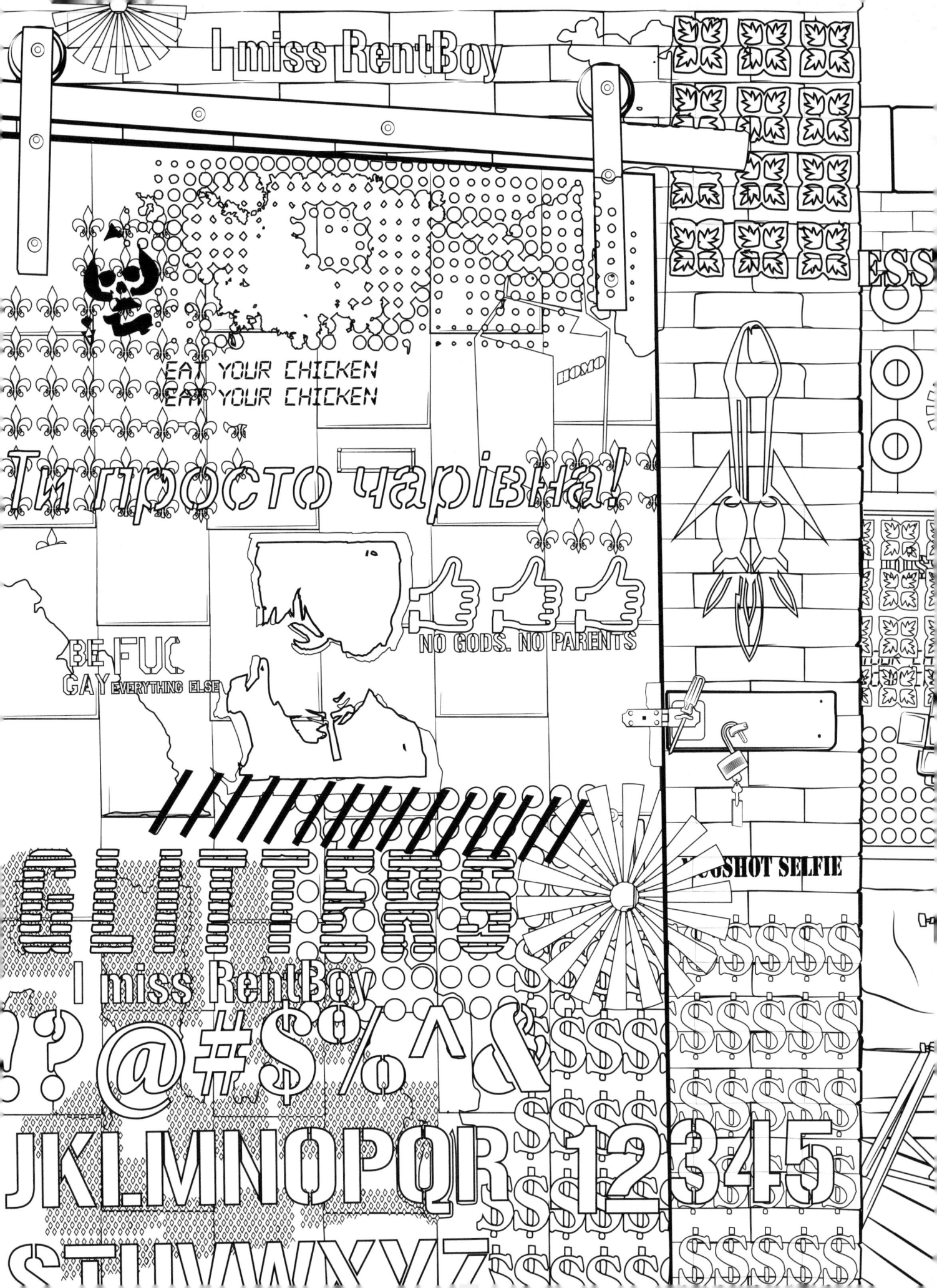
I miss RentBoy
EAT YOUR CHICKEN
EAT YOUR CHICKEN
Ти просто чарівна!
NO GODS. NO PARENTS
BE FUC
GAY EVERYTHING ELSE
I miss RentBoy
?? @#$%^&
JKLMNOPQR 12345
STUVWXYZ

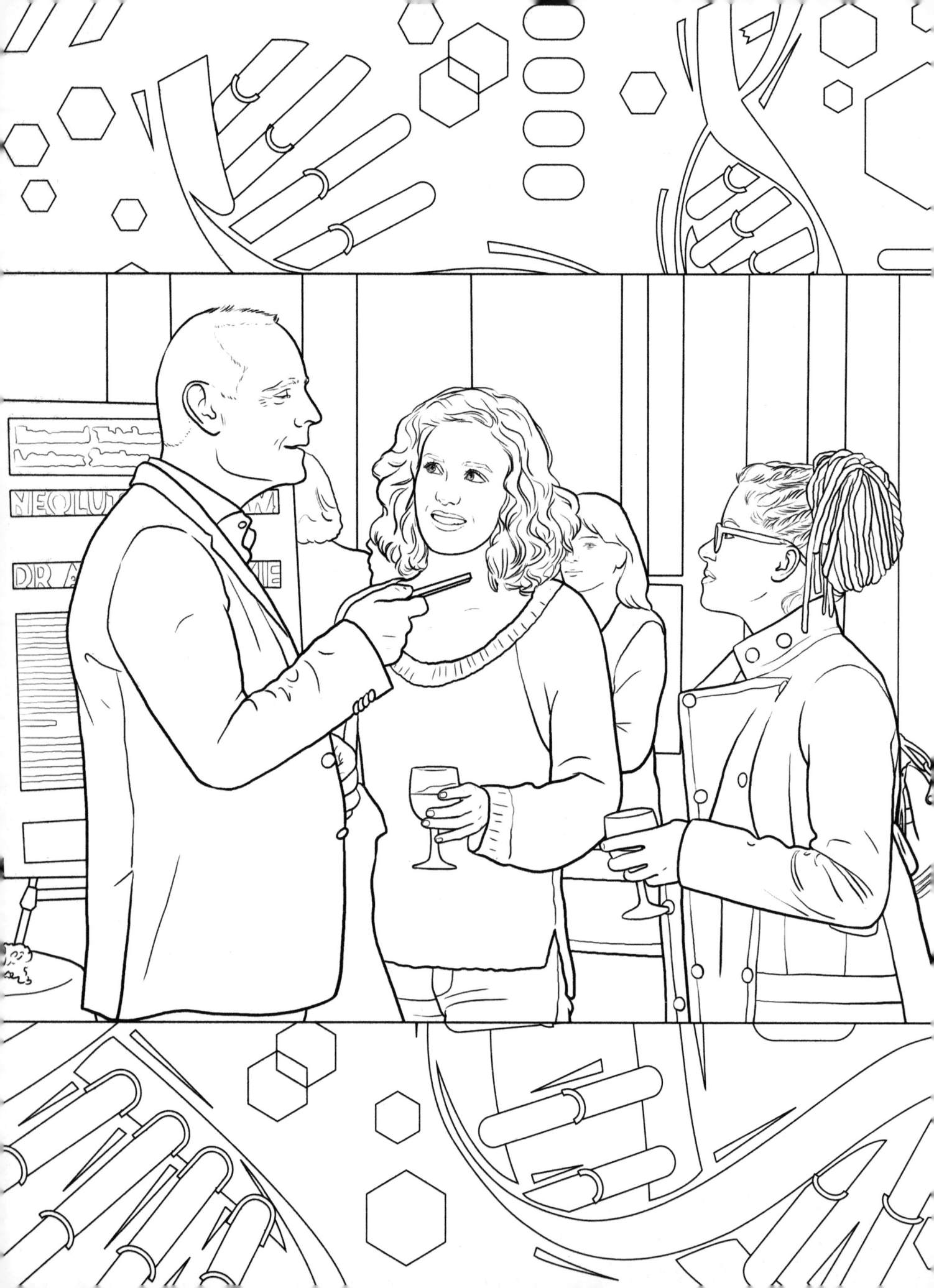

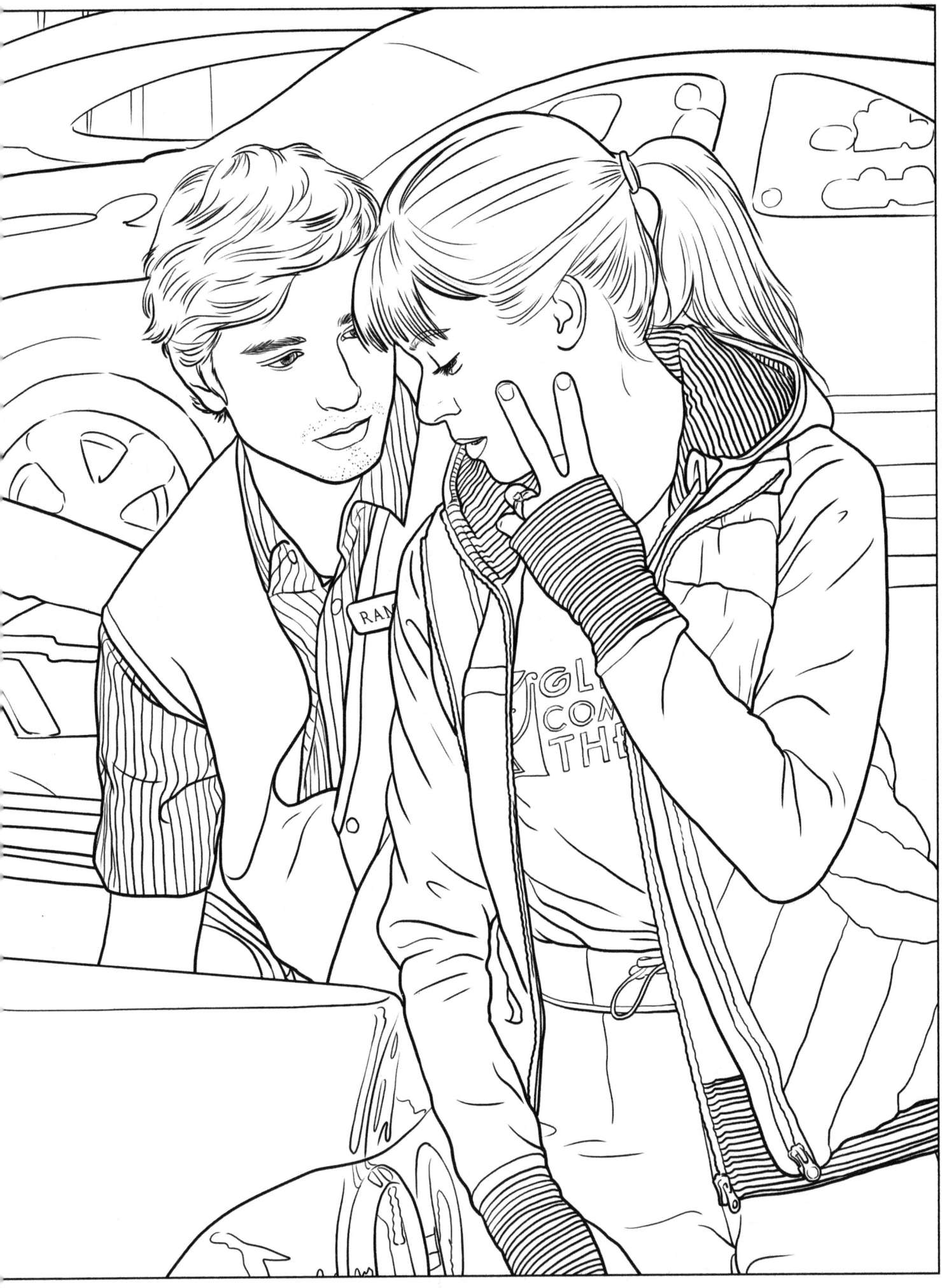
RAN

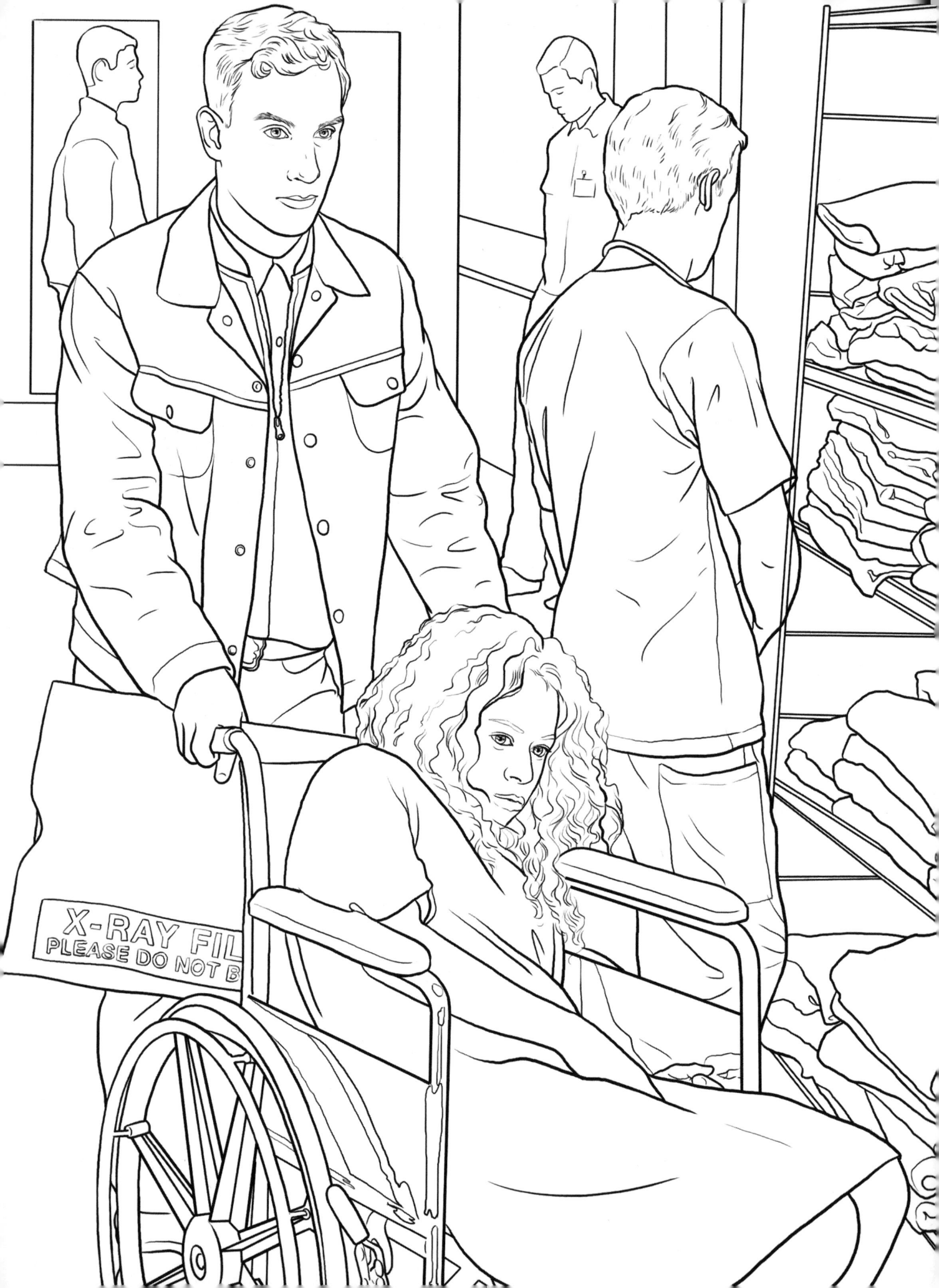
X-RAY FIL
PLEASE DO NOT B

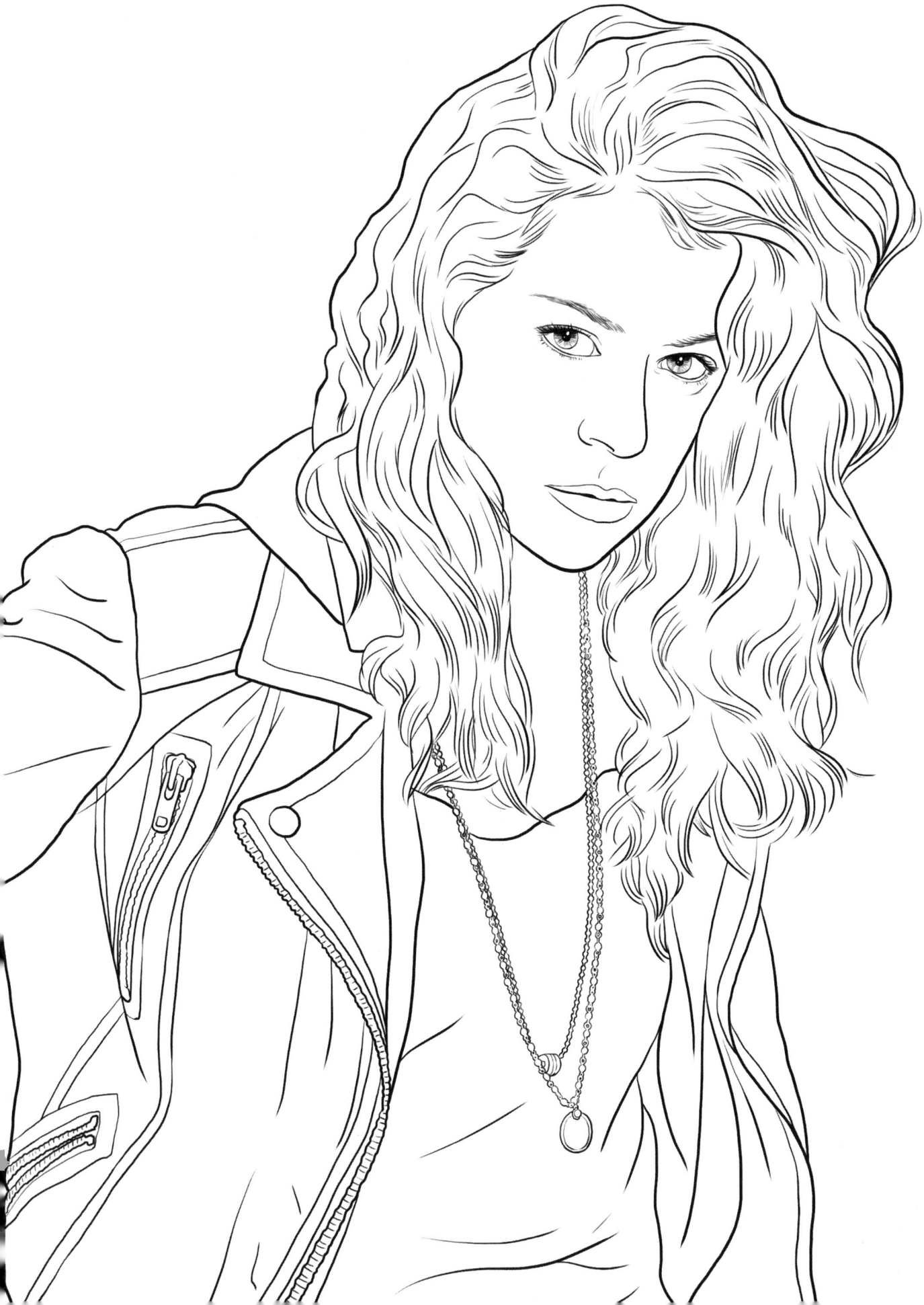

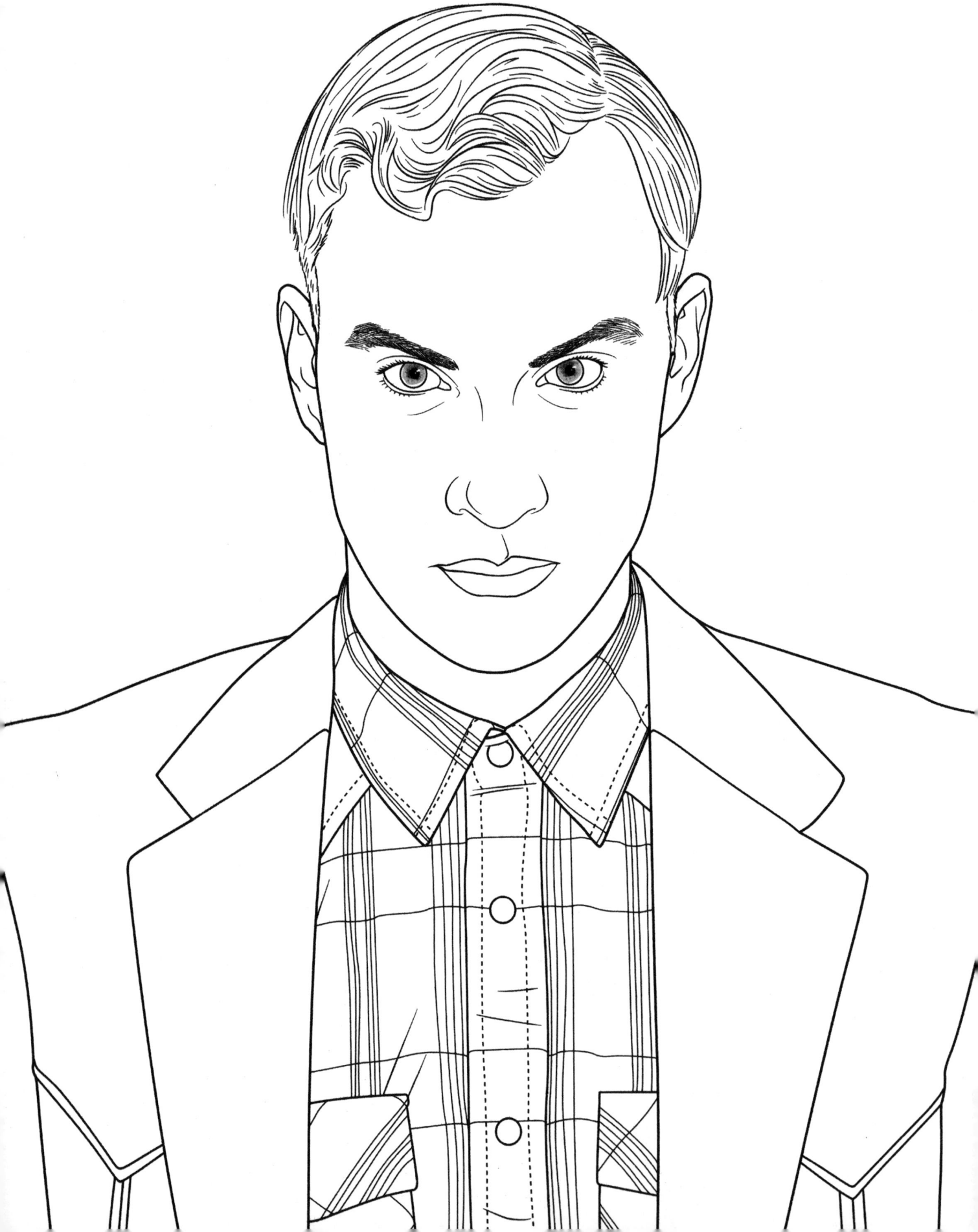

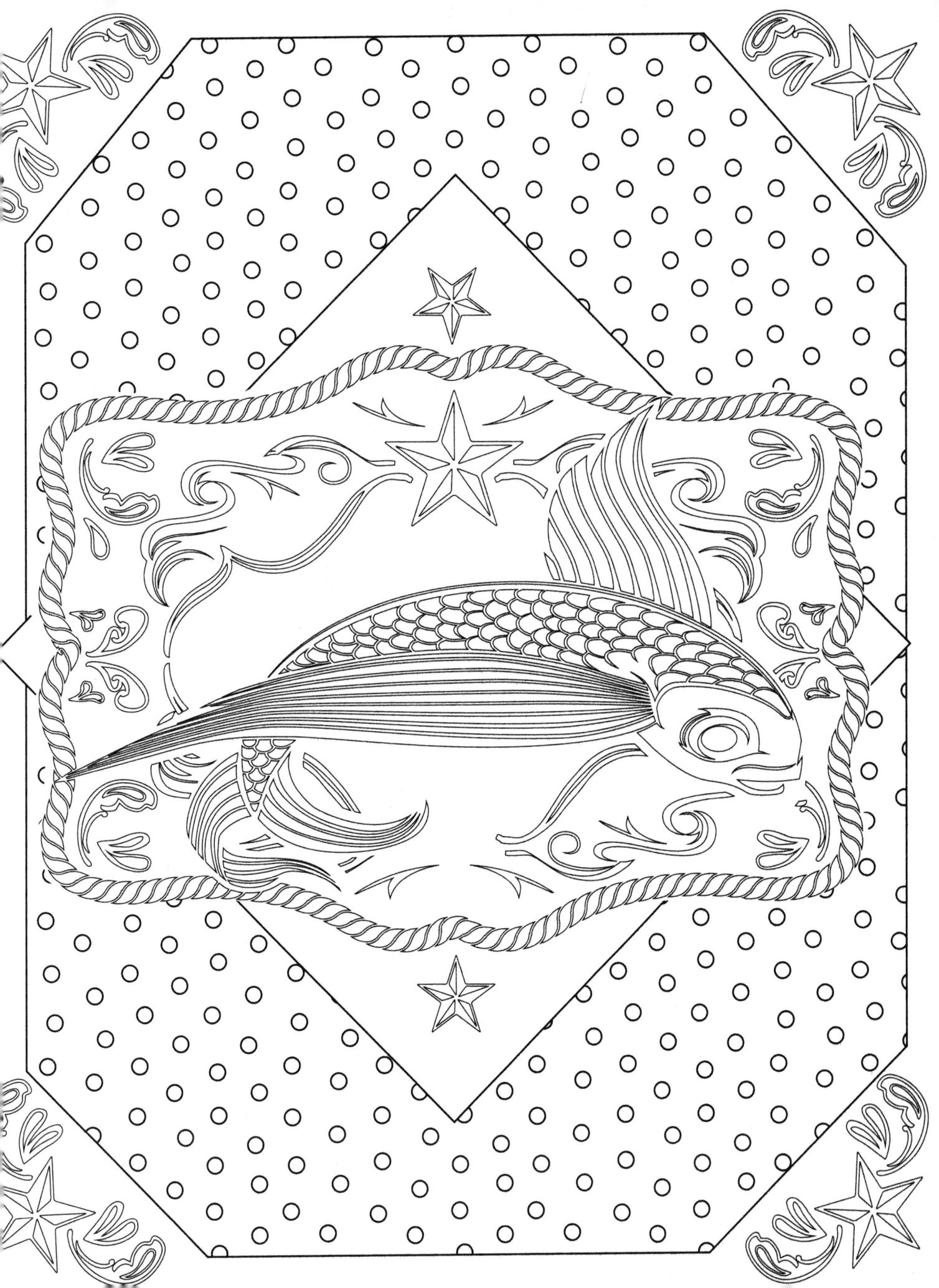

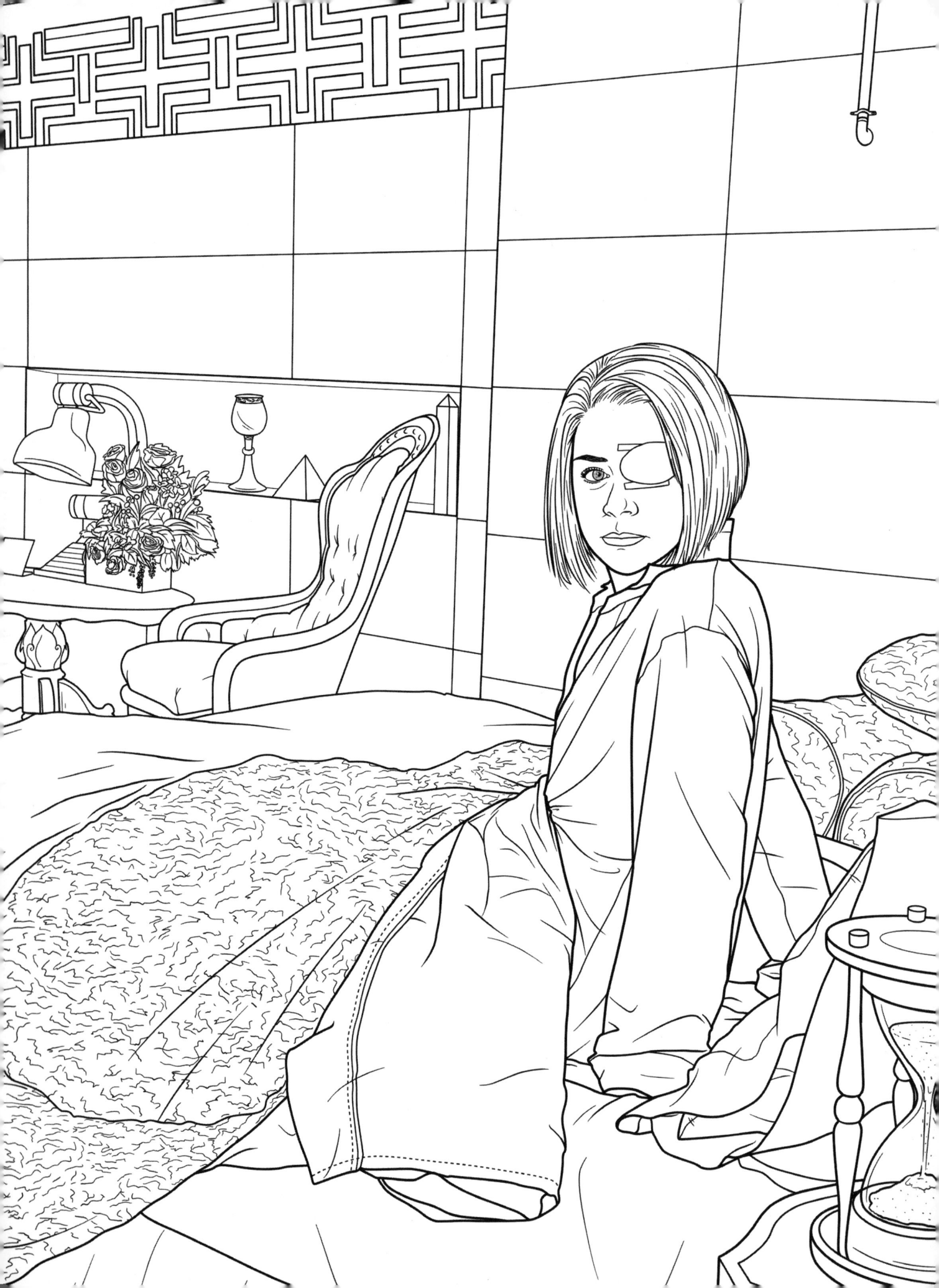

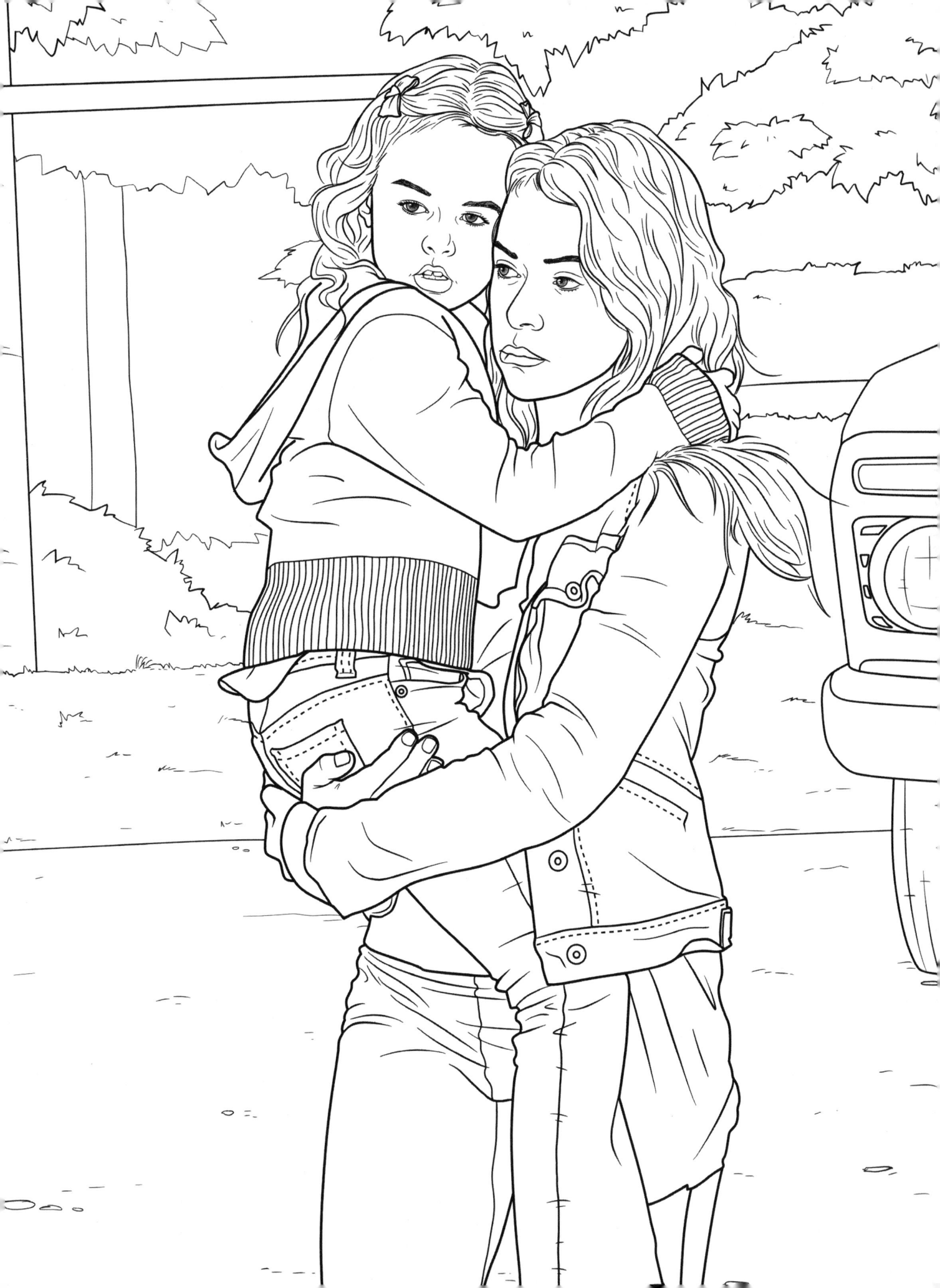

NEOLUTION:

The New Science of Self-Directed Evolution

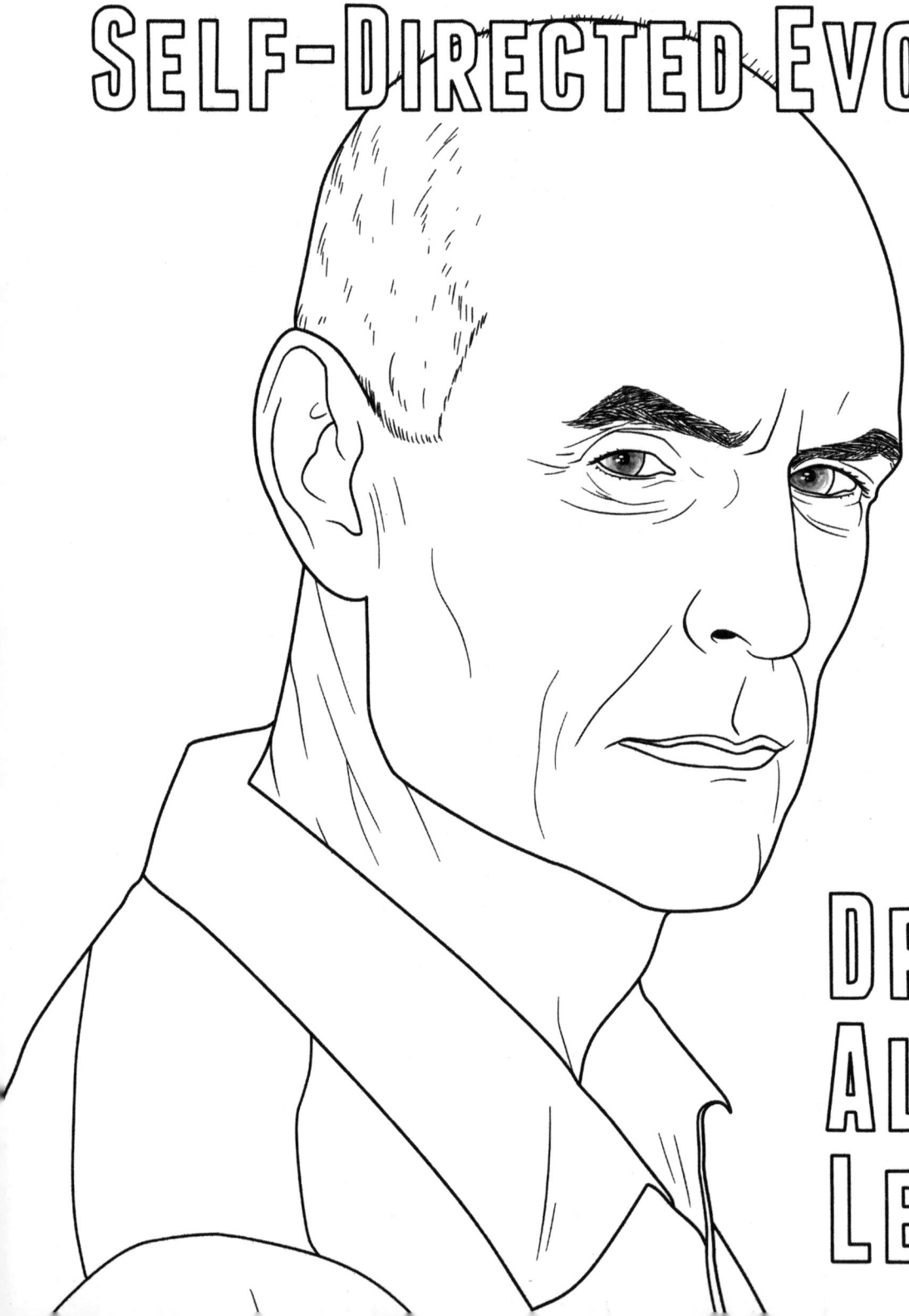

Dr. Aldous Leekie

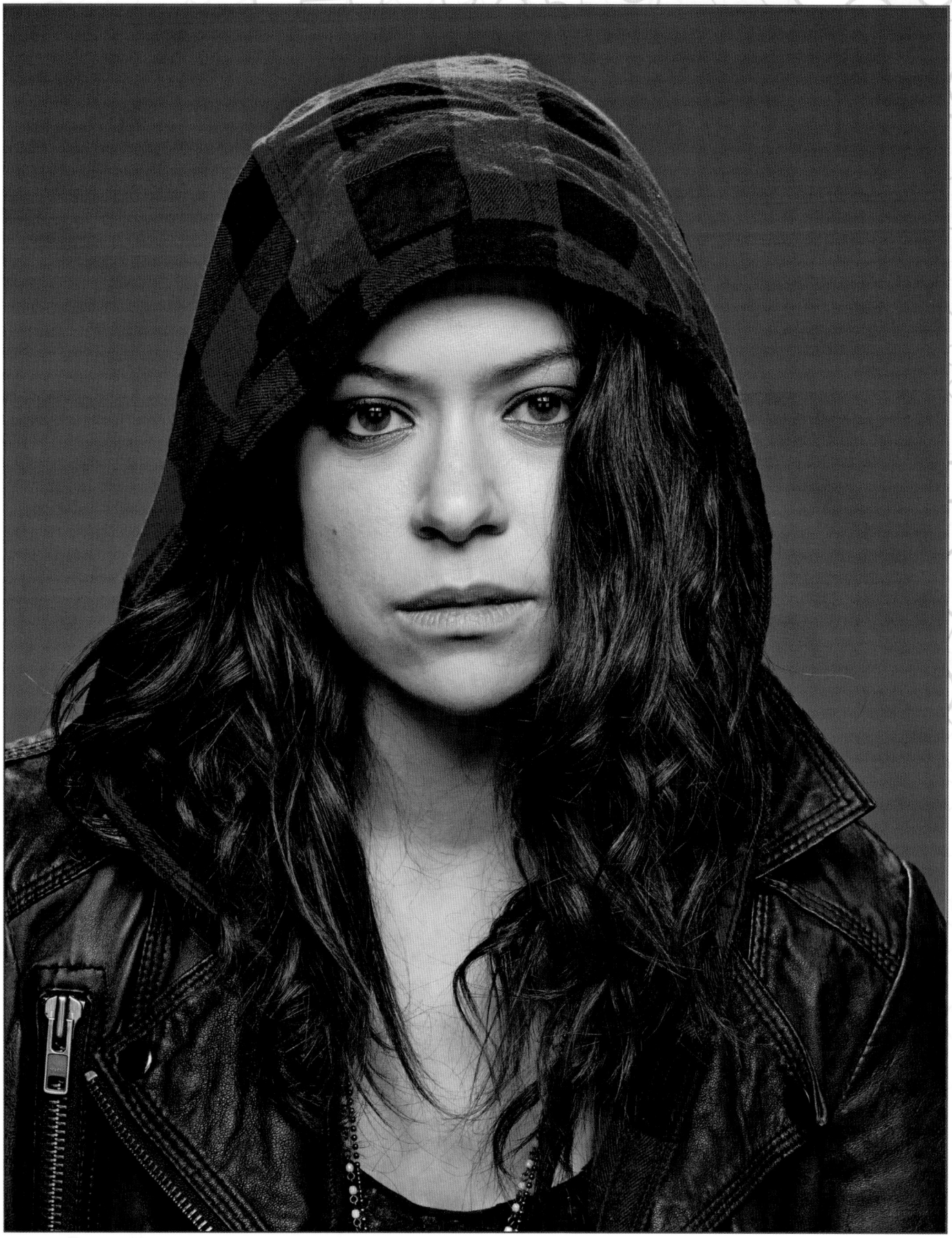

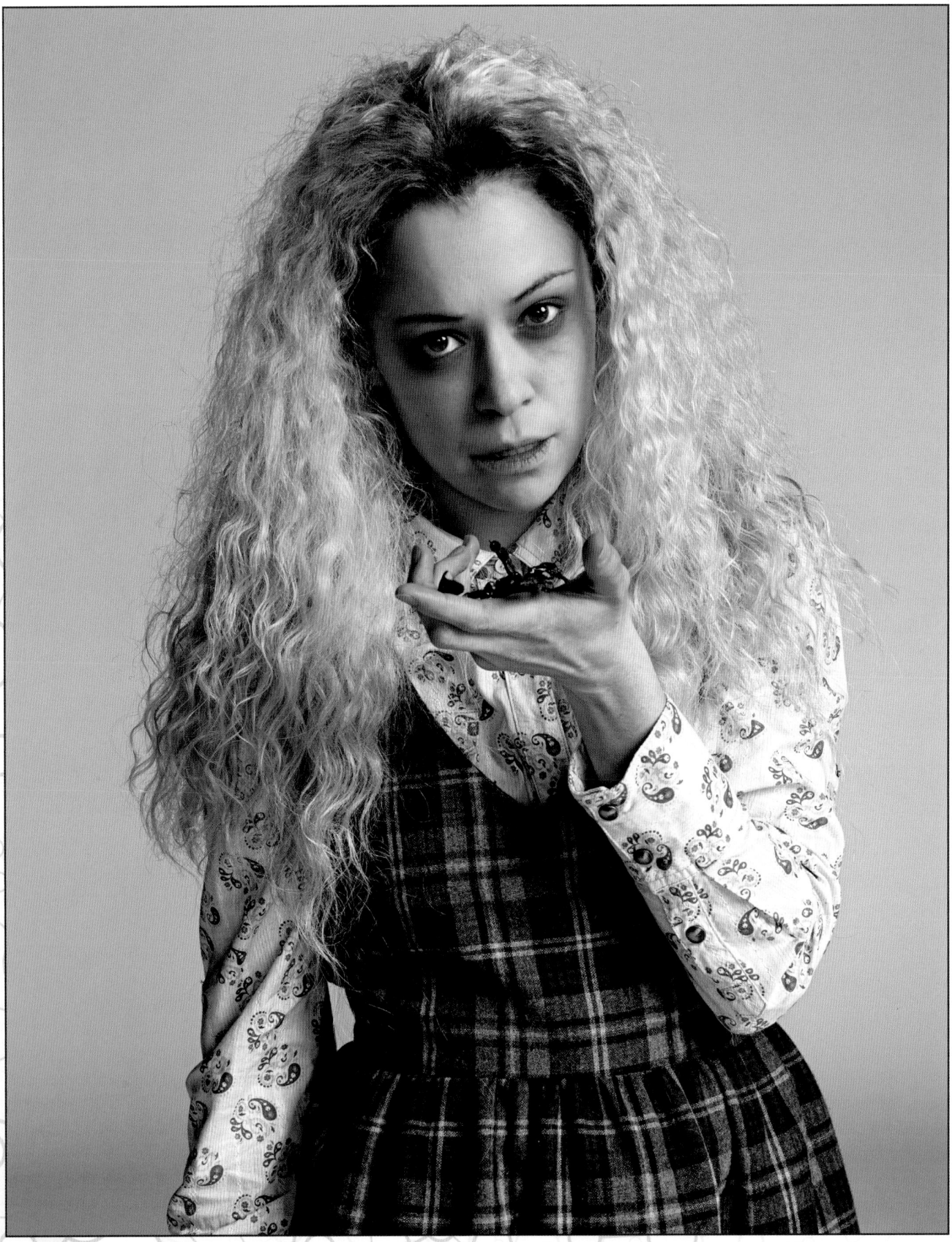

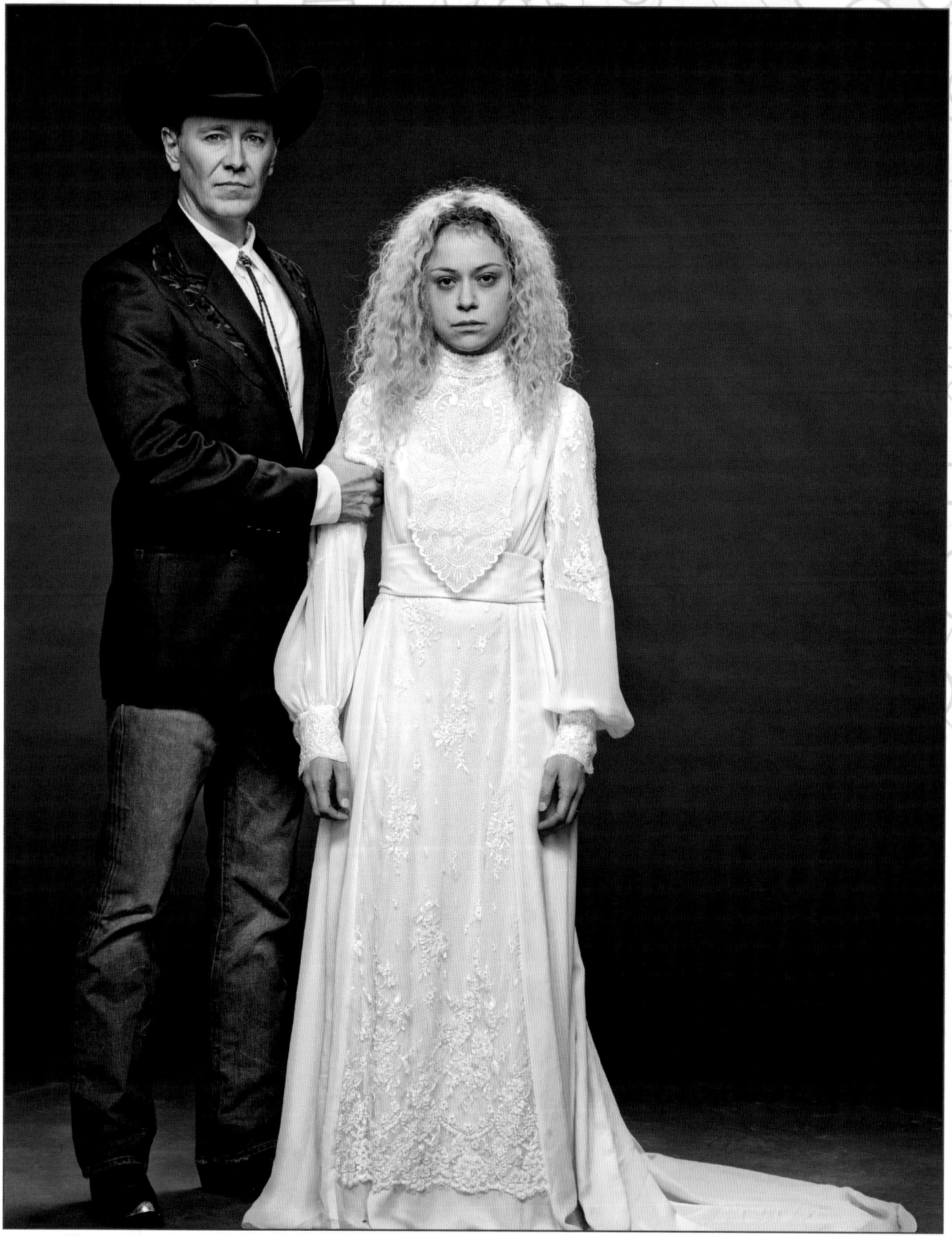

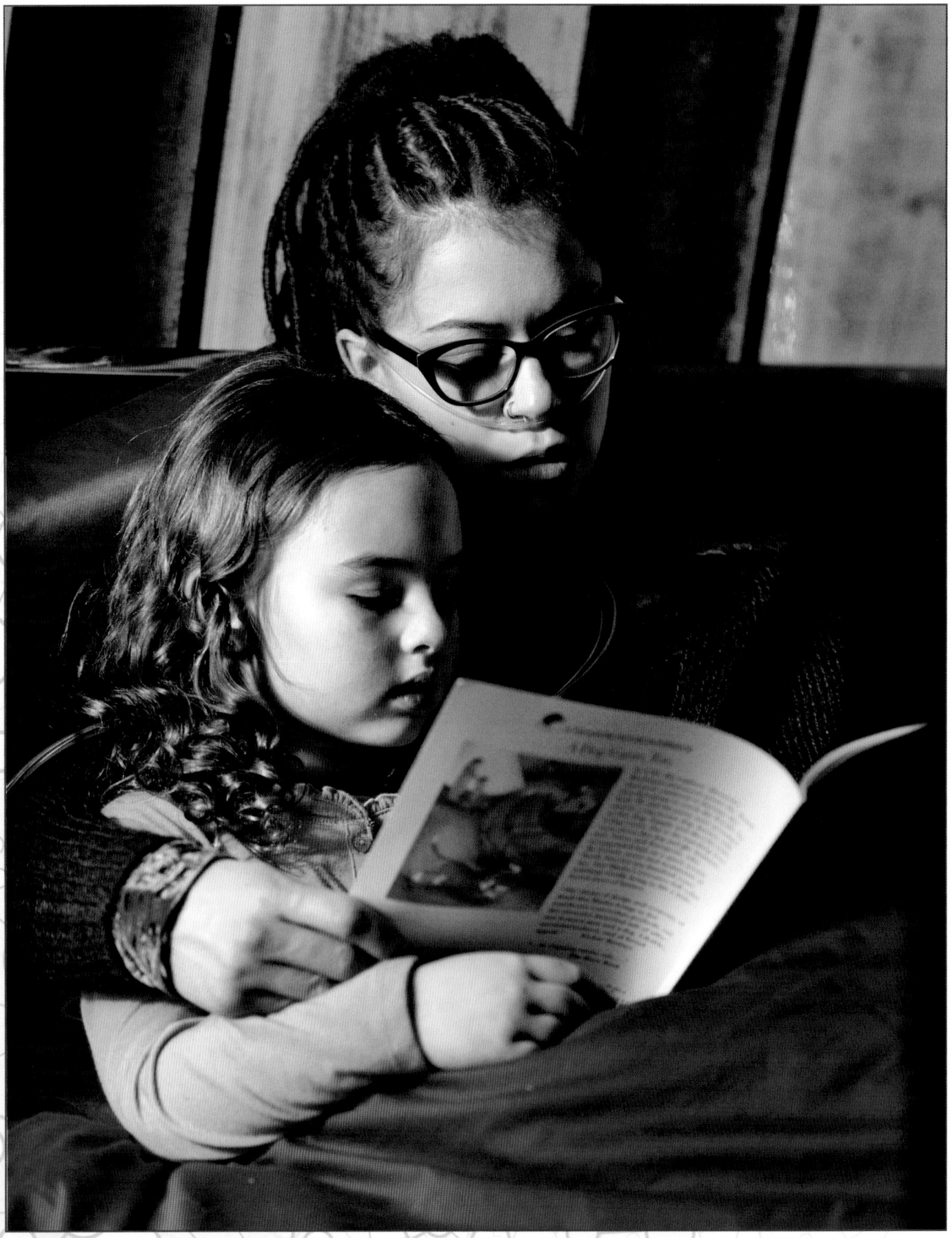

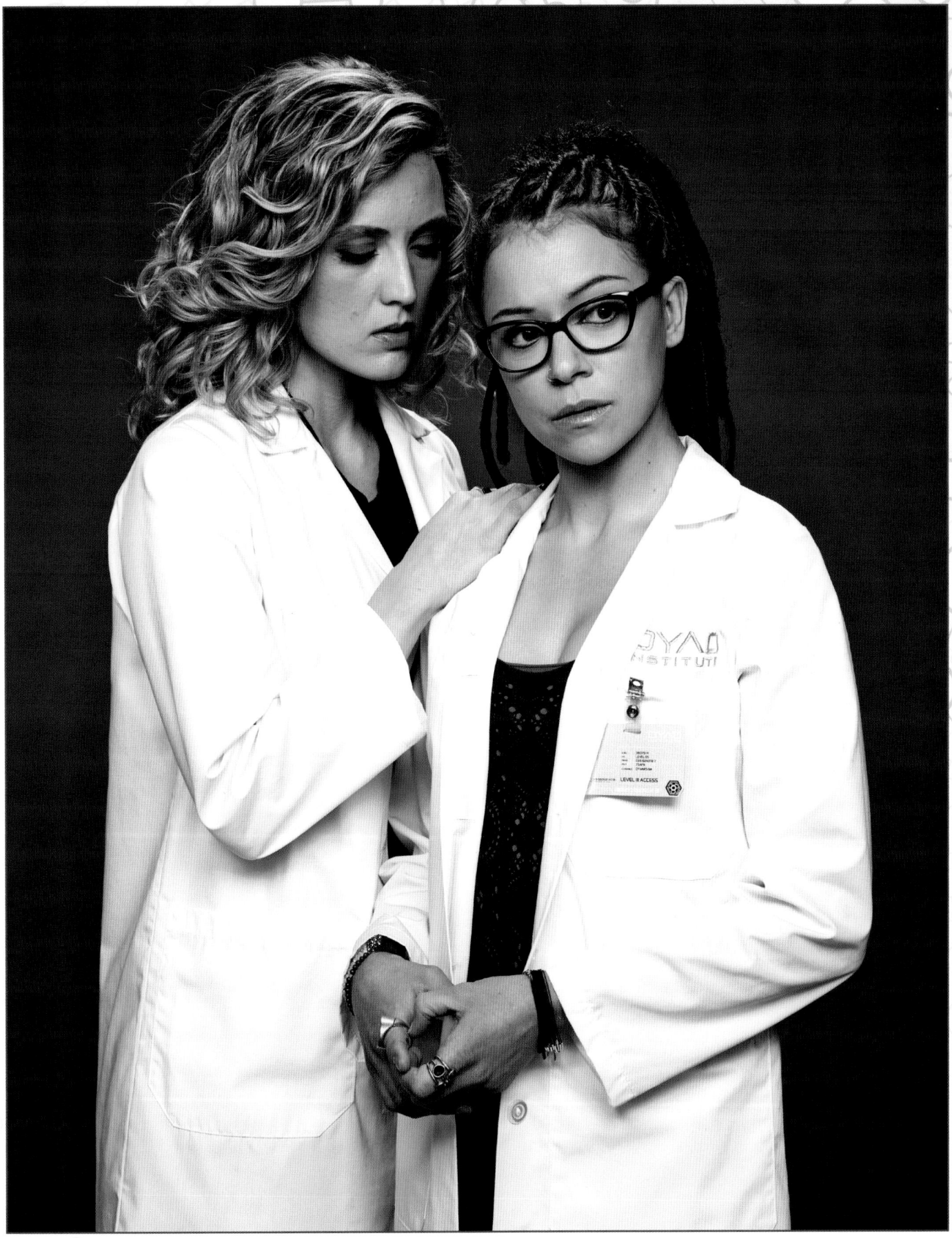
LEVEL III ACCESS

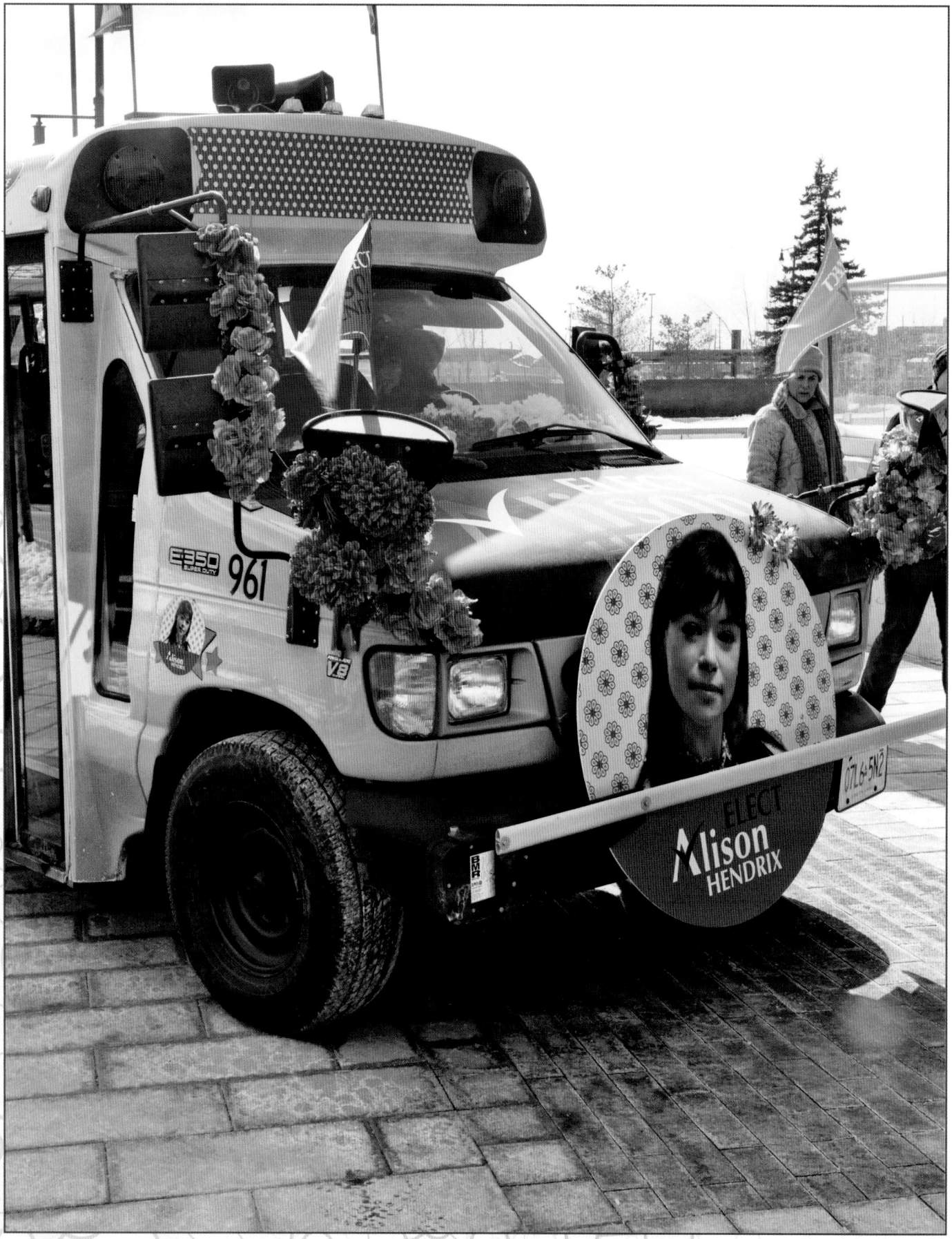
E350
SUPER DUTY
961
ELECT
Alison
HENDRIX

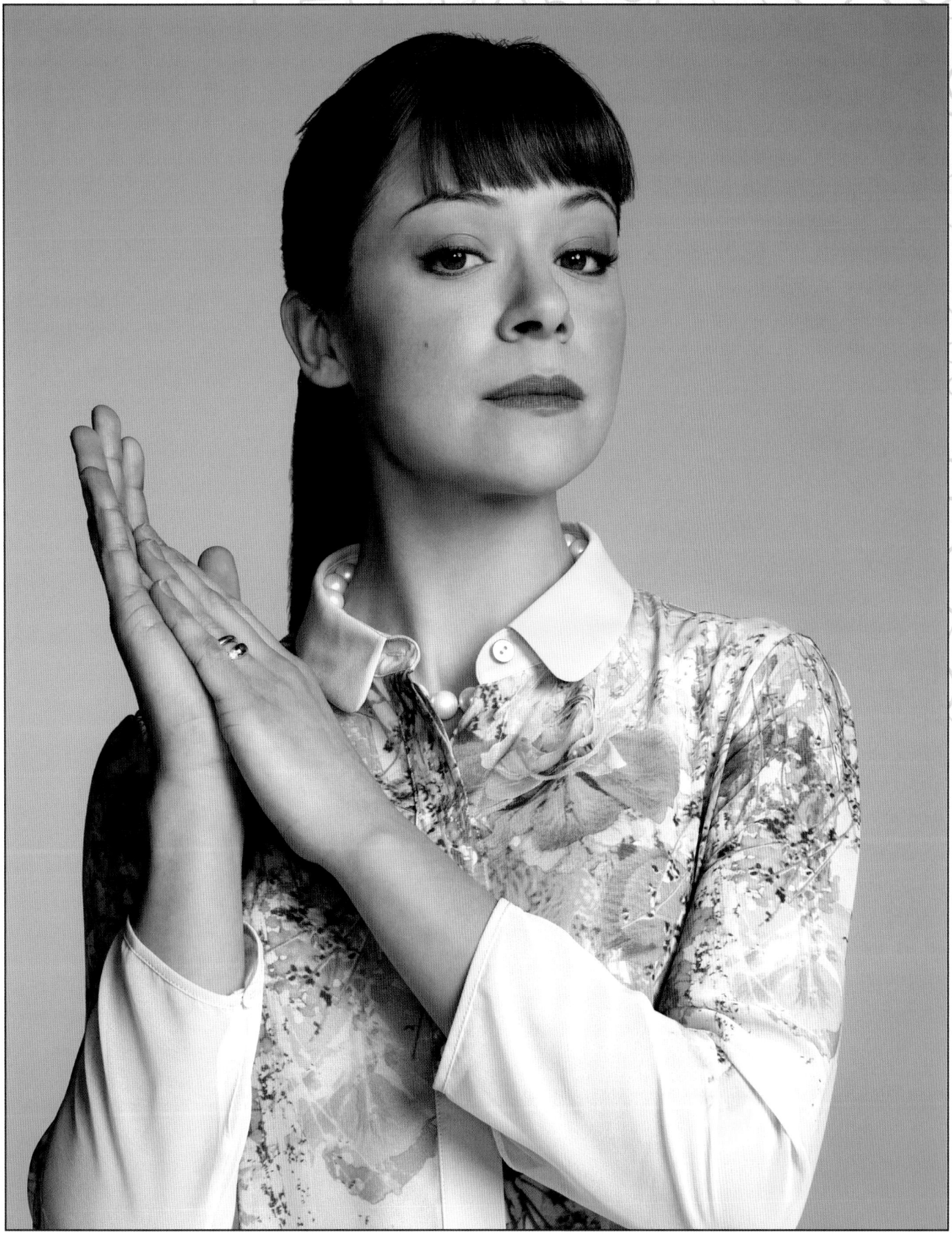

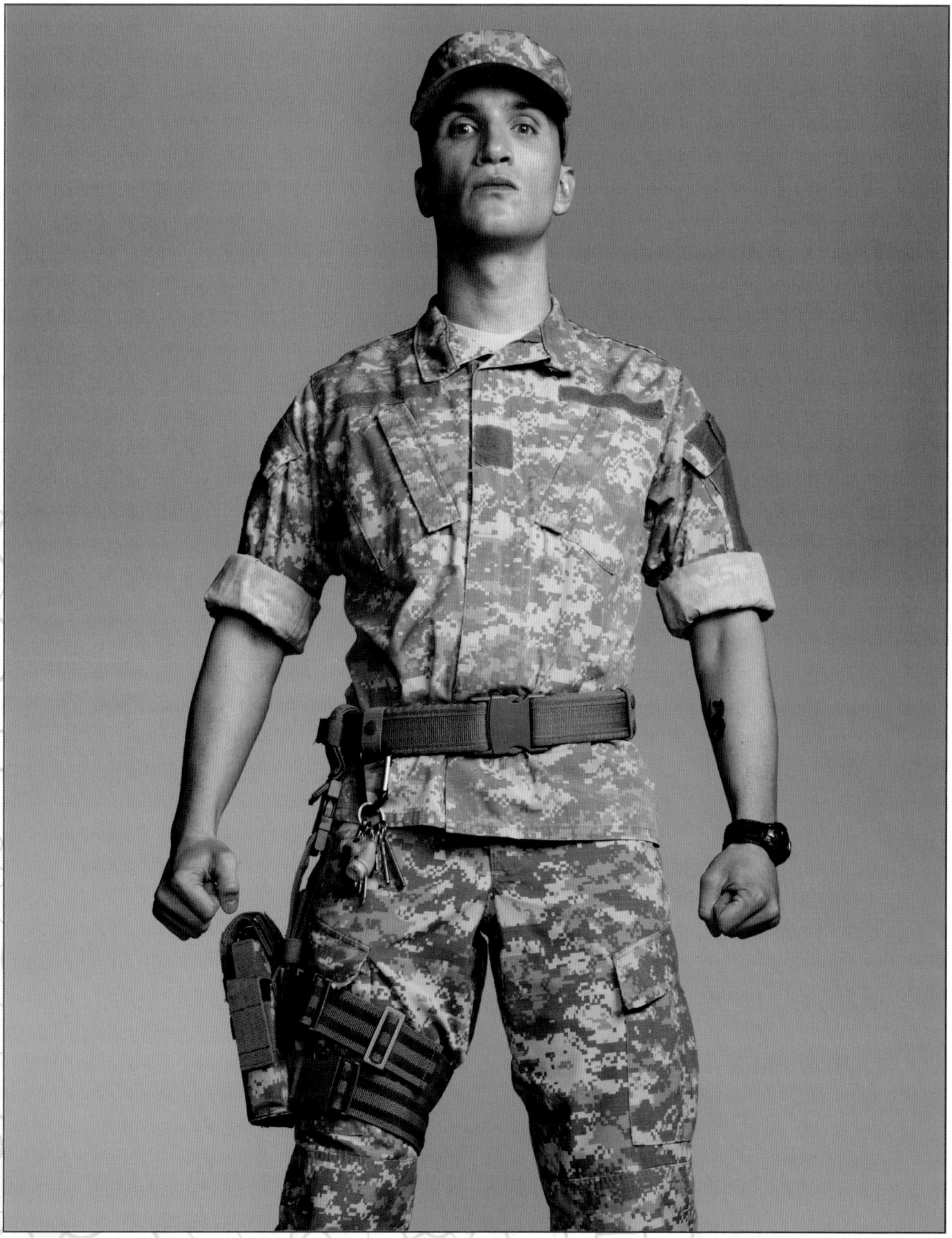

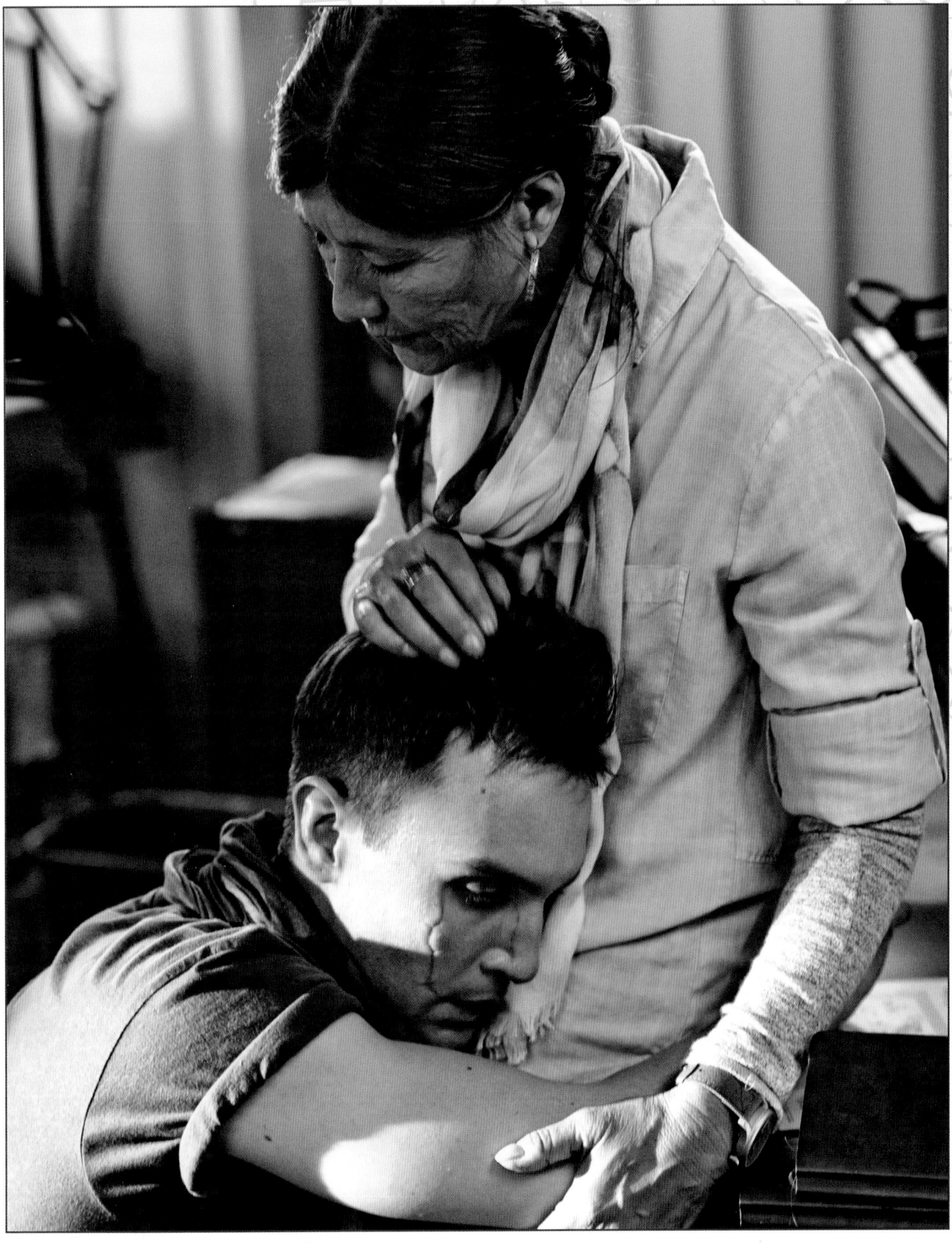

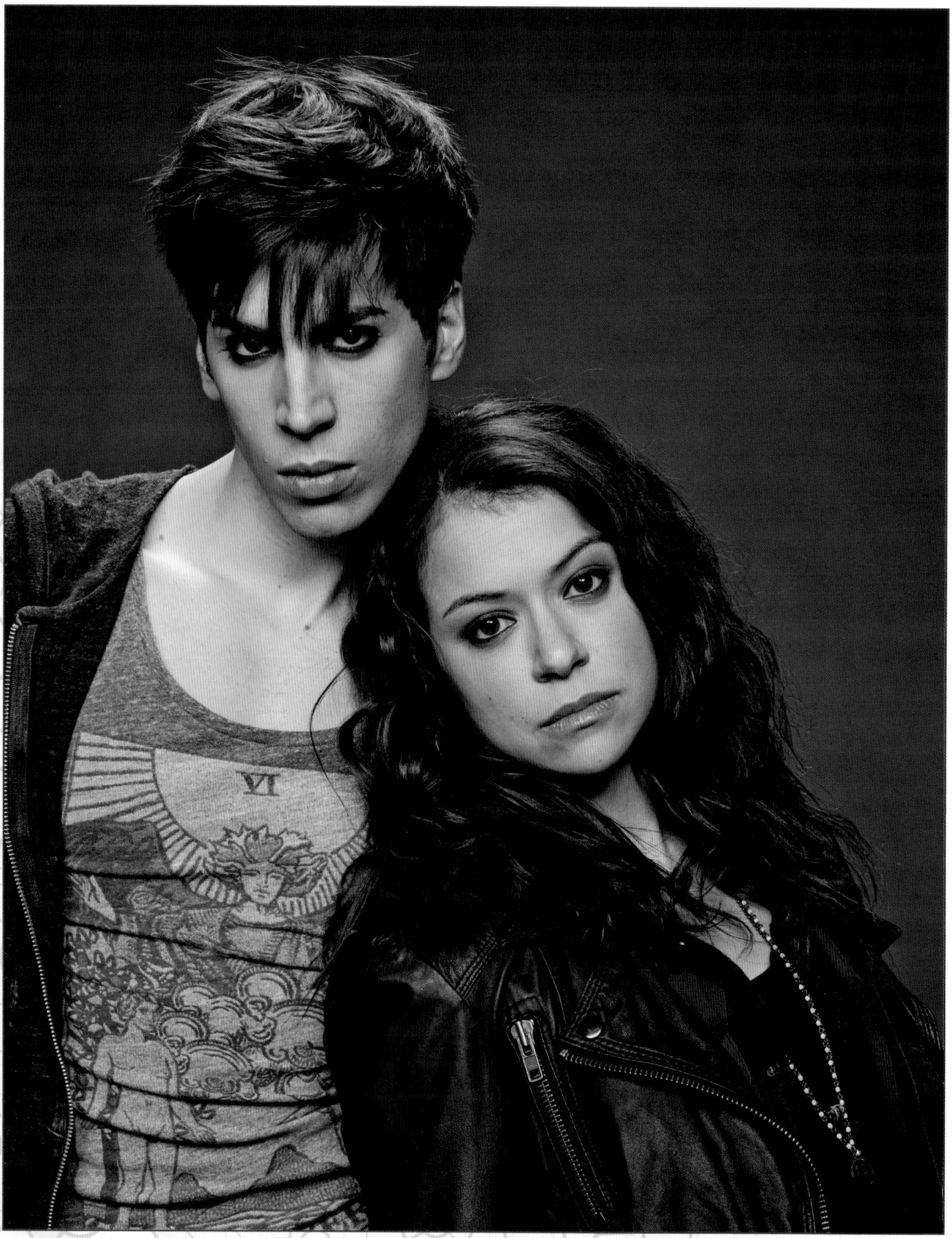
VI

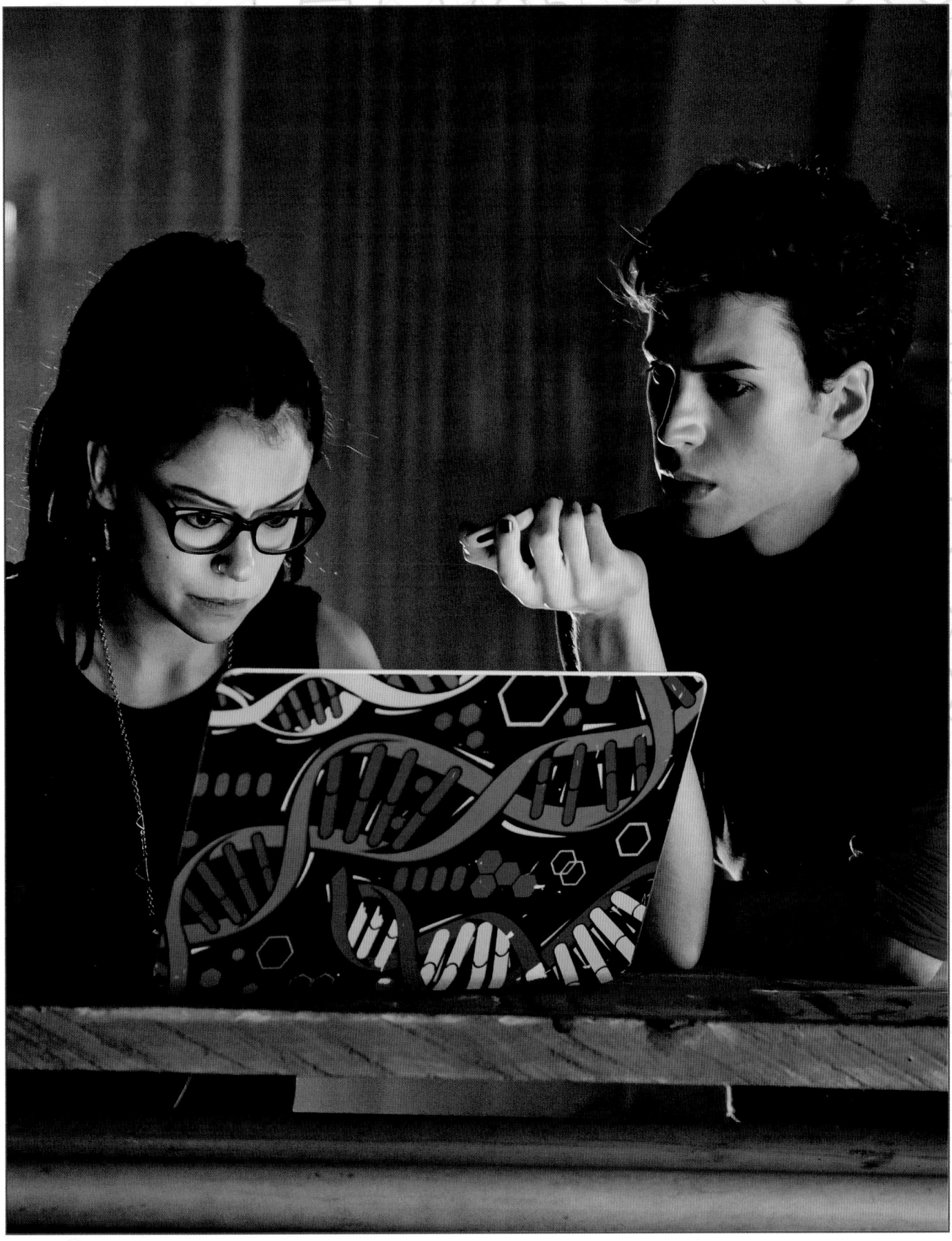

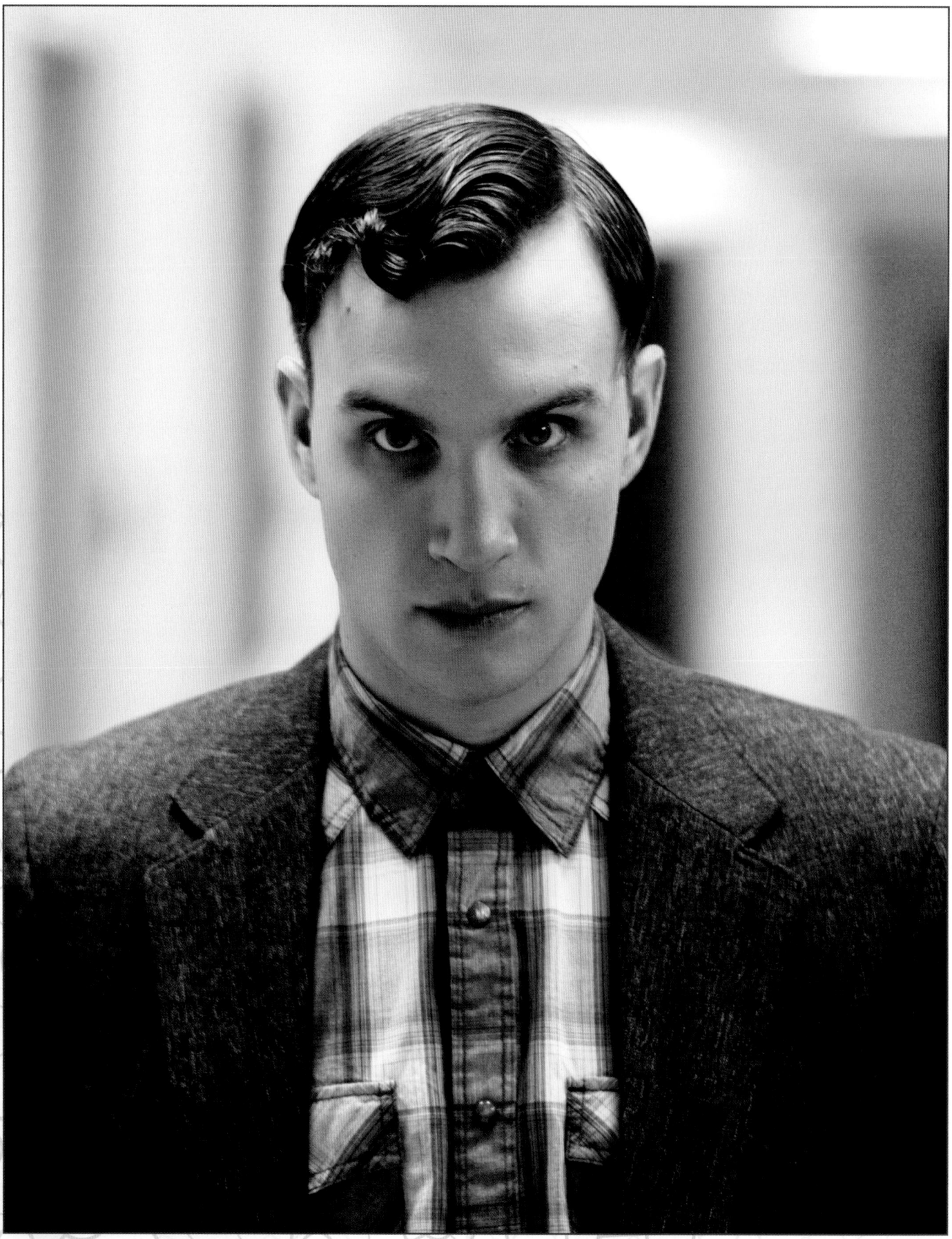

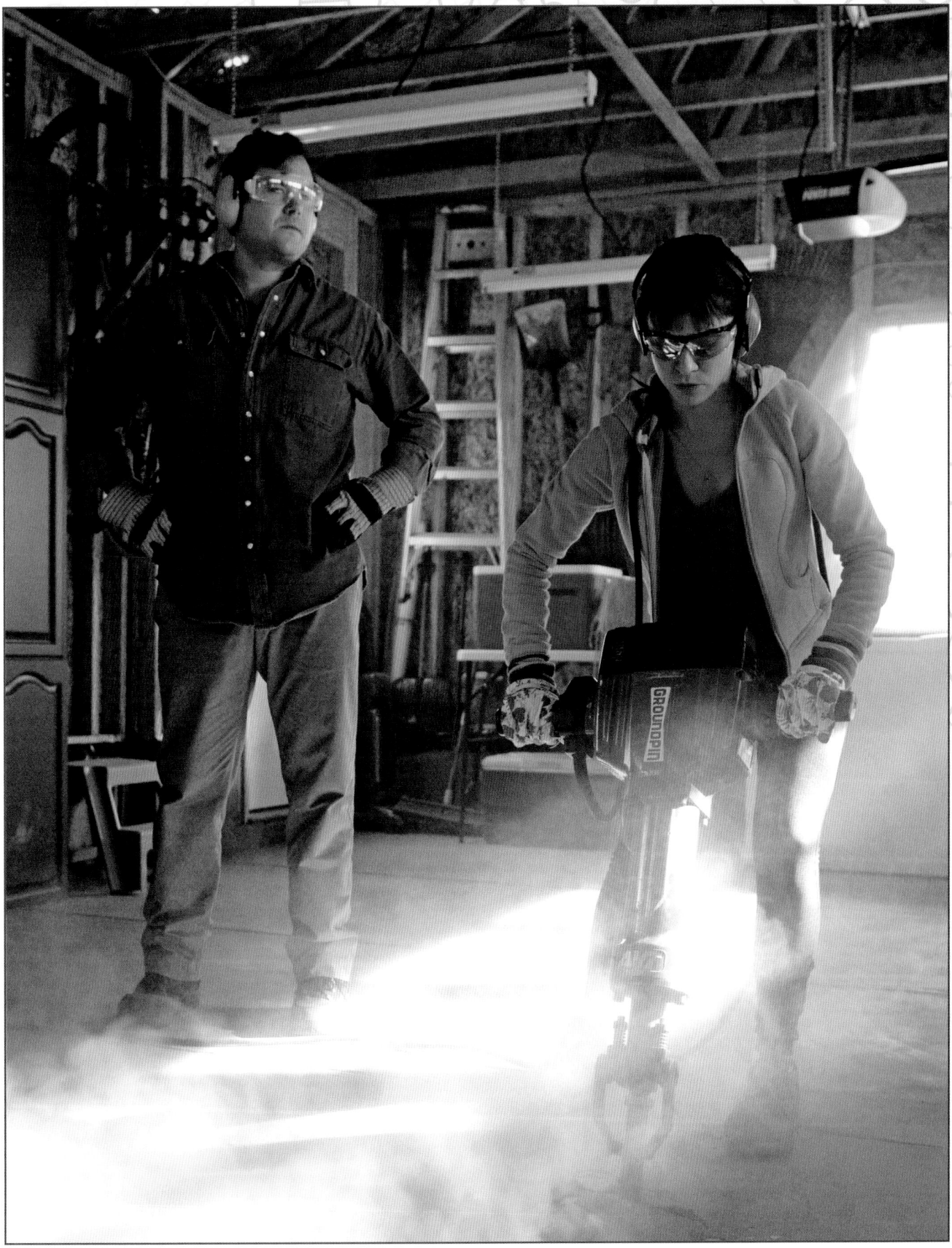
GROUNDPIN

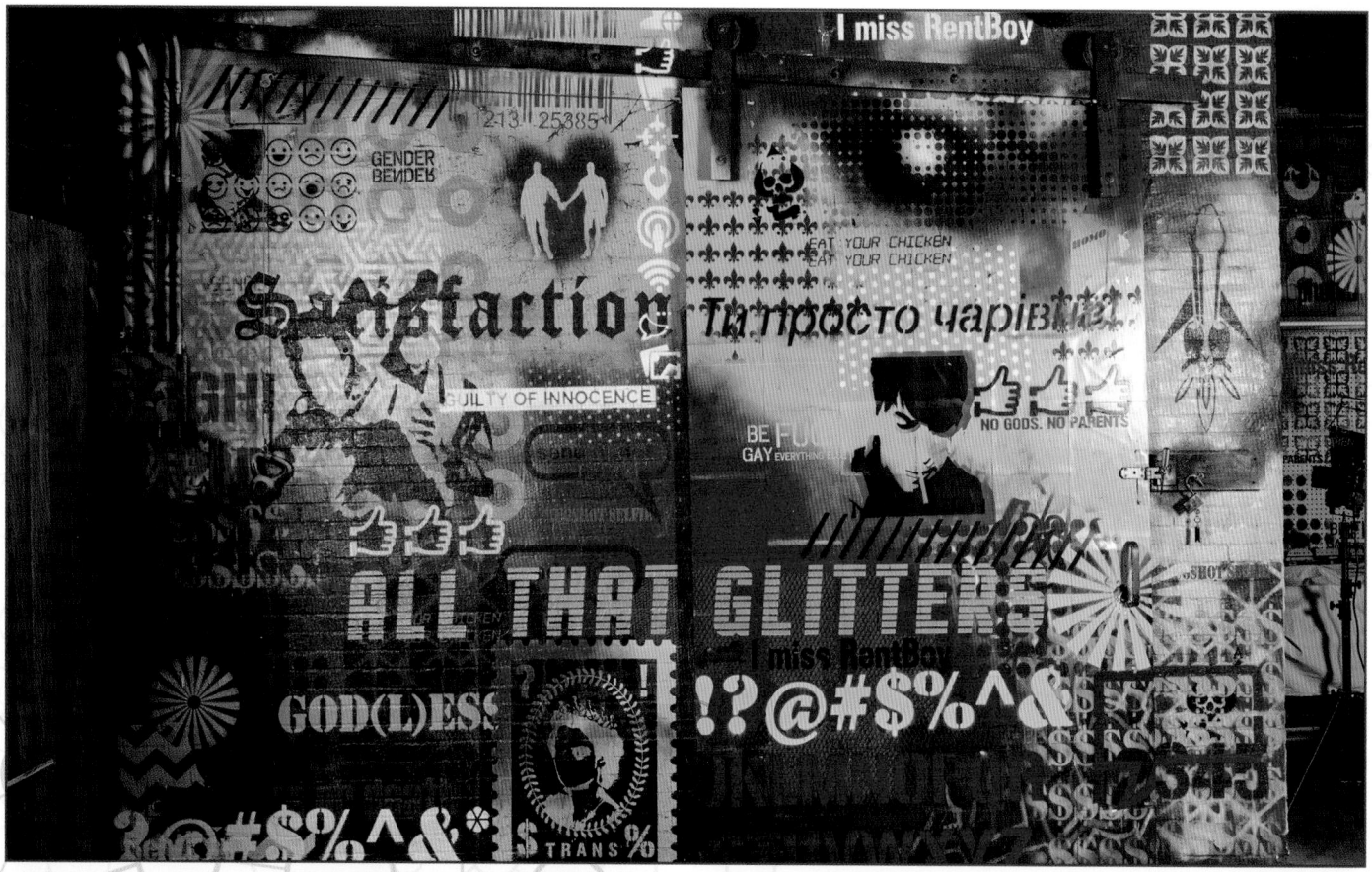
I miss RentBoy
GENDER BENDER
EAT YOUR CHICKEN
EAT YOUR CHICKEN
Satisfaction
Ти просто чарівн
GUILTY OF INNOCENCE
NO GODS. NO PARENTS
ALL THAT GLITTERS
I miss RentBoy
GOD(L)ESS
!?@#$%^&
TRANS

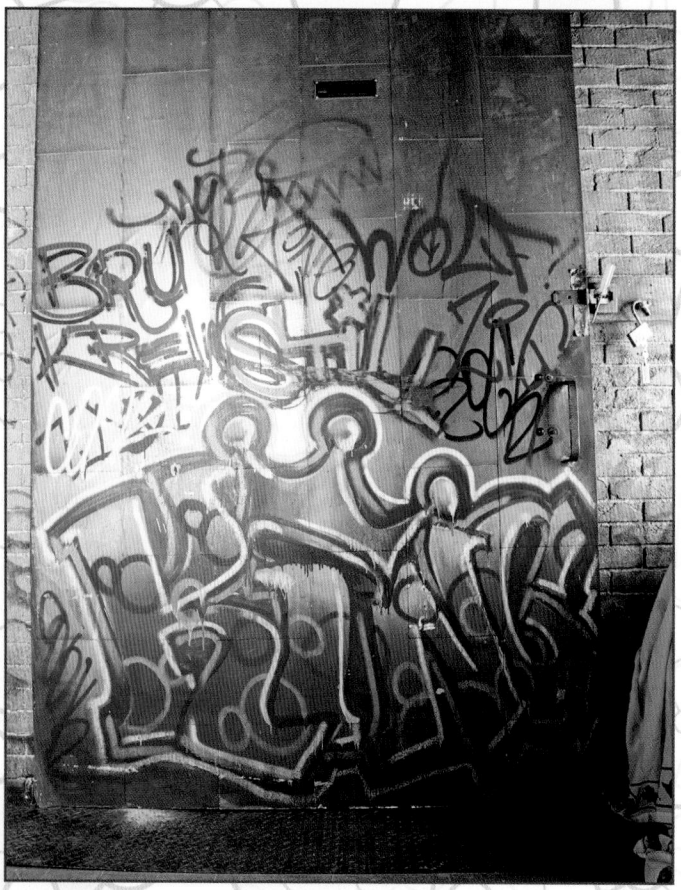

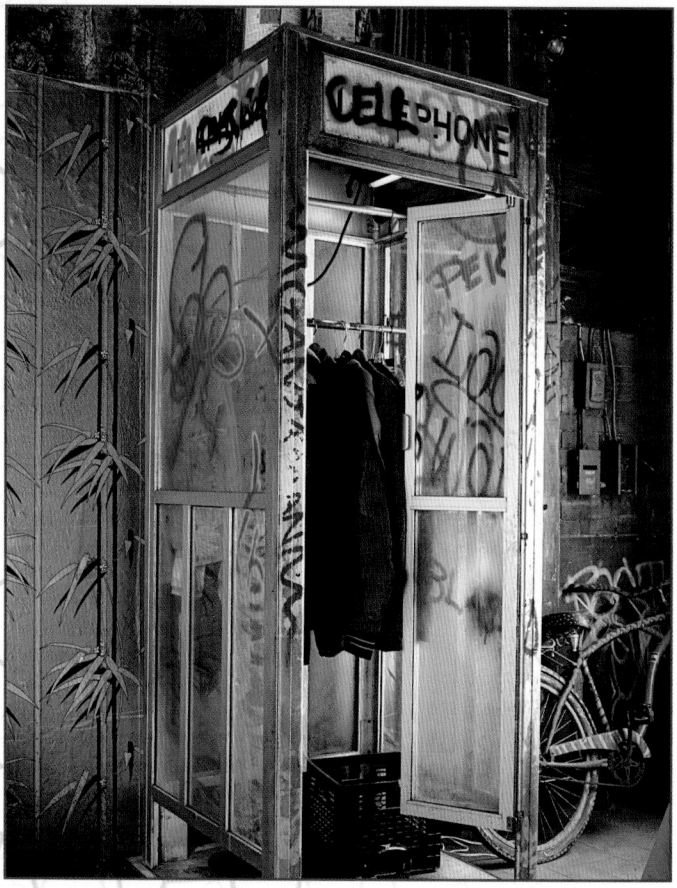
CELL PHONE

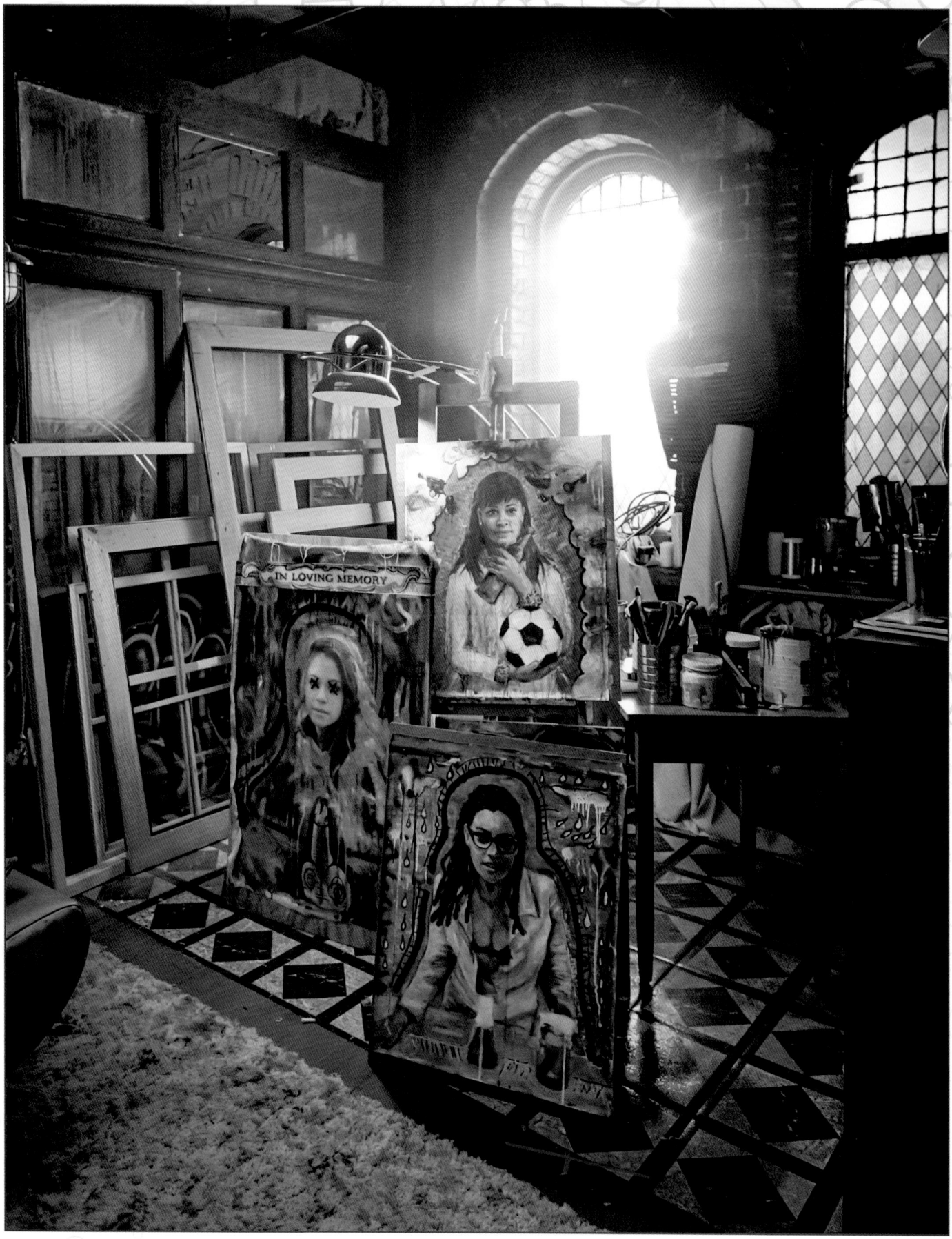
IN LOVING MEMORY

INSIGHT EDITIONS

PO Box 3088
San Rafael, CA 94912
www.insighteditions.com

Find us on Facebook: www.facebook.com/InsightEditions
Follow us on Twitter: @insighteditions

BOAT ROCKER
BRANDS

© 2017 Orphan Black Productions Limited.

All rights reserved.

Published by Insight Editions, San Rafael, California, in 2017. No part of this book may be reproduced in any form without written permission from the publisher.

Library of Congress Cataloging-in-Publication Data available.

ISBN: 978-1-68383-100-6

Publisher: Raoul Goff
Acquisitions Manager: Robbie Schmidt
Art Director: Chrissy Kwasnik
Designer: Leah Bloise
Project Editor: Kelly Reed
Production Editor: Rachel Anderson
Production Manager: Alix Nicholaeff
Editorial Assistant: Erum Khan

—

Illustrations by Adam Raiti, Robin F. Williams, and Pablo Matamoros

ROOTS of PEACE REPLANTED PAPER

Insight Editions, in association with Roots of Peace, will plant two trees for each tree used in the manufacturing of this book. Roots of Peace is an internationally renowned humanitarian organization dedicated to eradicating land mines worldwide and converting war-torn lands into productive farms and wildlife habitats. Roots of Peace will plant two million fruit and nut trees in Afghanistan and provide farmers there with the skills and support necessary for sustainable land use.

Manufactured in China

10 9 8 7 6 5 4 3 2 1